Kind Dynamite

Six Ways Women Can Use

Our Uniquely Explosive Power

to Persuade in Meetings

Kind Dynamite

Six Ways Women Can Use Our Uniquely Explosive Power to Persuade in Meetings

DR. KAREN LISKO

Niche Pressworks
Indianapolis, IN

Kind Dynamite™: Six Ways Women Can Use Our Uniquely Explosive Power to Persuade in Meetings

Author Photograph by: Sarah Hoag Photography

Published by Niche Pressworks; NichePressworks.com
Indianapolis, IN

ISBN
Paperback   978-1-962956-61-1
Hardback   978-1-962956-62-8
eBook   978-1-962956-63-5

Library of Congress Control Number: 2025904367

The views expressed herein are solely those of the author and do not necessarily reflect the views of the publisher.

To the badass women who came before us
who weathered being mislabeled as aggressive
when what they were really showing us
was what it looked like
to be assertive.

TABLE OF CONTENTS

CHAPTER 1

The Case for Kind Dynamite

I was sitting in my office in Phoenix, scanning the *New York Times* to take a breather from writing some tricky jury selection questions for an upcoming trial, when I came across an article that set off alarm bells in my head. The title read: "Women Know Exactly What They're Doing When They Use 'Weak Language.'"[1]

Then I began to read the article itself and came across this passage:

> It's outrageous that women have to tame their tongues to protect fragile male egos, but the likability penalty is still firmly in place. The solution [is]...to normalize "weak language" as a strong way to express concern and humility. If we do that, we won't have

to keep encouraging women to communicate more forcefully.[2]

Wait. What? I thought.

Shock coursed through me. The title spoke directly to my decades-long research in language and women's power, but the message was stunning — and wrong.

I felt my shoulders tense in frustration and dismay as I reread the paragraph. I assumed the author meant well — and I was sure he was trying to help women deal with the unique challenges they face — but the message was not only depressing, it was also mostly based on outdated research studies. Had I been reading this article in 1990 or 2000, I might have been nodding my head in agreement. But it was 2023.

As if the outdated research wasn't bad enough, when I read the comments, my shock and dismay shifted to worry. So many online readers gave the article a thumbs up — and many of those thumbs were the beautifully manicured ones of women!

The irony was that I'd just told one of my clients something completely different only days before, which mirrored advice and research I've relied on to prep amazing clients like the two women I helped prepare for their appearance on the TV show *Shark Tank*.[3] (More on that in a moment.)

That article made me realize that although women have made so much progress in communicating assertively, we still have much work to do — including confronting these outdated mindsets that continue to disempower us. Because unfortunately, those mindsets still linger, and I see them in my clients every day.

The Fear Mentality

As a coach and social scientist who teaches assertive communication, I encounter so many impressive women in my work who tell me they hold back in meetings. They say things like:

- "I don't speak up because I'm afraid my idea isn't novel enough."
- "I don't speak up because I'm likely to get shot down — or interrupted — by someone else in the meeting."
- "I don't speak up because I don't feel like I can organize my thoughts well enough in an on-the-spot response."
- "I don't speak up because I'm more junior on the team and don't think it's my place."
- "I don't speak up because I don't feel it will make any difference."

And the grandmother of them all:

- "I don't speak up because I'm concerned I'll make someone in the conversation feel uncomfortable (and often, that someone is me)."

Have any of these thoughts ever circulated in your brain?

Have you ever experienced a tug-of-war in your head when you *knew* you had something of value to say yet debated with yourself about speaking up?

I'll confess that even though I teach assertive communication, I've had that internal battle too.

Often, when I ask my clients what holds them back from asserting themselves, the word *discomfort* enters the sentence. Some use the word *fear*.

How many times have you held your tongue instead of confronting someone about an issue (or worse, talked *about* someone rather than *to* that someone) and hoped things would resolve themselves, only to find that the problem never really went away? Have you spent more time mulling over your frustration, telling yourself what so many of our mothers told us: that if you don't have anything nice to say, you shouldn't say anything at all?

The unfortunate fact is that none of these coping methods address the true issues. As a result, we're left to suffer in silence instead of fully expressing ourselves as the capable professionals we truly are.

The Updated Good News About Women and Credibility

So, what is the updated reality about women and credibility?

My doctoral dissertation from more than 30 years ago studied powerful and powerless language in women and men.[4] Back then, two key findings were true:

1. Women who spoke in a powerful way were rated as more credible than women who spoke in a powerless manner.
2. Powerful women could not match the higher credibility assessments of powerful men.

I have continued my research since then. As a result, I know that *today*:

1. The first finding is still true.
2. The second one is most definitely false.

Ready for the great news? Recent research has found that women who portray a powerful speaking style are seen as *equally credible* as men.[5] Today, research is finding more similarities in men's and women's persuasiveness than differences.[6] I also work as a trial consultant, and my ongoing research in the human laboratory of the courtroom has provided the same evidence. In fact, women attorneys can enjoy a credibility advantage when they take a prominent role on male-dominated trial teams. That advantage also exists in the business world.

In addition, did you know that research also shows that reading or hearing stereotypes about our supposed powerlessness (ahem, the outdated research) can hurt women's self-confidence?[7] We don't need that.

We *must* stop believing this is our path as professional women. We *must* stop repeating this outdated assertion that women are not as credible as men. We *must* stop misinterpreting women's assertiveness as aggressiveness. Have you had that experience? Misinterpretation *can* happen, *and there are remedies for it.* The most common of these is to keep asserting and to keep supporting the women around you who are being assertive too. Of course, it's possible you may also need additional tools that *do not* require scaling back to "weak language" to help you more effectively assert your point.

It's time to focus on what's true (the current research). Not simply to be up to date but to throw out the negative messaging that keeps us trapped in unproductive mindsets. So, here's the deal. I'm *not* going to try to talk you out of your discomfort. I'm not going to tell you to simply get over feeling afraid. And I would be a liar if I told you that reading this book cover to cover will make you completely comfortable with speaking assertively.

The truth is that I'm going to urge you to *race toward* your discomfort by trying new, proven techniques I'm going to teach you, and by accepting that the consequence of speaking assertively and effectively sometimes means you will *still* feel uncomfortable before, during, and after you do so. I assure you, even though you may be uncomfortable, speaking assertively is still worth doing and just may be critical for you and for your colleagues.

The key to being effectively assertive lies in understanding how to combine the two crucial elements that make up what I call Kind Dynamite™.

What Is Kind Dynamite?

Let's set aside the research studies for a moment. They don't tell the full story.

We are living the full story.

I coach powerful female executives to amplify their authentic voices both through their messaging and through their demeanor. I have conducted decades of research on people's perceptions of women in the courtroom and in the conference room.

The findings are clear. They are consistent. Professionals trust and want to follow female executives who speak with a combination of compassion and power. Think of it as compassionate directness. *That* is Kind Dynamite.

> **This is my bold promise to you:** In this book, I will equip you with *concrete, powerful* ways to *speak what's on your mind* with compassionate directness in a way that is persuasive and, at key moments, quotable. And I will teach you to do so with the Kind Dynamite balance of not minding what others think while presenting with others in mind.

Assertive Talk Using Kind Dynamite Begins in Your Mind

I did my doctoral training in all the external ways we project confidence and made that my life's work. I could coach women to look confident like nobody's business! And then, over several years (I never claimed to be a quick study), I finally figured out that external confidence just doesn't stick *unless* you begin internally.

My *Shark Tank* clients are a perfect example.

Sharp young entrepreneurs Becky App and Abby Jordan had a novel idea to take a "not your ordinary ice cream business" national. Their business, eCreamery, had already found modest success, but they needed more capital to keep growing their vision. Their deep belief in their concept of making exceptional ice cream personalized for the recipient and shipping it nationwide moved them to apply for a spot on the hit reality television show *Shark Tank*. This long-running show invites entrepreneurs to pitch multimillionaire "Sharks" to invest in their startup businesses.

My clients got accepted to be on the show and were told they'd have two minutes to pitch their idea to the Sharks, and they had to be great. That led them to call me.

When we initially practiced their pitch, I assessed their approach and determined they were much too stilted. It seemed they were thinking too much and "being" too little. So, I asked them how they pictured their approach on camera.

"We want to be seen as businesswomen who are kind and approachable," Becky said.

Abby agreed. "We certainly don't want to be seen as bossy bitches who no one would want to build a partnership with."

They were worried about seeming too aggressive on the one hand and not being taken seriously on the other. They thought they had to choose between being personable and being professional.

My first job was to talk them out of that either-or mindset. I'd already noticed they were more effective when they were brainstorming and debriefing with each other *in between* their prepared remarks. We just had to capture that energy and ease within their presentation.

Coaching them was easy. They already had the Kind Dynamite ingredients; they just needed to change their minds about who they should be during their pitch.

Becky and Abby aren't alone in this respect. I've coached hundreds of clients, and *they* have taught *me* something fascinating: To be assertive, most of us need to make a single decision. That decision is to give ourselves *permission* to be assertive when we might ordinarily filter what we say — and to show up with warmth when we do so.

Throughout this book, I'll tell you more about how Becky and Abby applied the Kind Dynamite principles to go from budding entrepreneurs to gaining so much credibility on *Shark Tank* that their sales increased *1,200 percent*.

All the things we worked on together carry benefits you will also enjoy:

- You will feel better about asserting yourself.
- You will feel less resentful of those prone to interrupting.
- You will break out of patterns you were perhaps taught at an early age — hold your tongue, be polite, wait to be called on — that, unfortunately, mute your voice and your power.

Speaking to Others Using Kind Dynamite Will Impact Their Behavior

How often have you opted not to speak out because you believed it wouldn't change anything? That belief is simply not true.

Remember the saying, "If you don't have anything nice to say, don't say anything at all"? Consider another alternative: If you don't have anything nice to say, *think of a better way to say it.*

I'm going to provide you with ways to do exactly that. Even if you think speaking up won't change the person you're speaking to or the circumstances, asserting yourself *will* change *you*. You will feel proud of yourself. And you might just begin a process of change for others. In a meeting setting, the person you positively impact might be someone observing your assertiveness and taking your approach as a model for their own behavior.

Here are some likely outcomes you can look forward to by learning and practicing these skills:

- You will be interrupted less. Powerless communication invites more interruptions. That will not be your path.
- You will be expressly positioned to grab the floor back if you lose it momentarily.
- Your colleagues will remember your point longer than those of others who fail to use the explosive combination of compassion and power from Kind Dynamite.
- Others will notice a difference in your assertiveness, even if they can't put their finger on what it is that has changed in your communication.
- You will have fewer kick-yourself moments that come from staying silent only to have someone else voice the same point circulating in your head.

Even if you don't get your way the first few times trying these techniques, you will have begun the process.

And the opportunity for impact extends beyond you to potentially benefit all women. Inequities still exist between women and men — financially, politically, and socially, to name a few. In fact, The World Economic Forum Report notes it could take up to 268 years to close the economic gender gap.[8] Since none of us will be alive to celebrate that event, we might as well get busy doing our part now to close it. And we will close it more quickly if we communicate with power.

An Exercise in Assertive Humility

Many of my clients are attorneys, so they'd tell me it's time for a disclaimer right about now!

So, how does assertive humility play into defining the boundaries of this book? It's important to own where the limitations lie and to do so without apology. In this instance, there are two.

This book will not (and should not) pretend to speak to a world view of communication. We are too diverse to pretend one size fits all in persuasion. The research I cite and my recommendations here are very WEIRD. That is, they are oriented around Western Educated, Industrialized Rich Democracies.

Researchers have pointed out that only 12 to 17 percent of the world's population resides in WEIRD countries, yet 96 percent of social psychology research is conducted with this population.[9] In particular, the vast majority of these studies have been conducted in the United States, and more recent research has found that this narrowly focused trend has not improved.[10] Please keep this in mind for your particular situation and application. Your results may differ depending on many variables.

Fortunately, research about persuasion in other parts of the world is out there. In her book, *The Culture Map*, Erin Meyer makes a powerful case for differences in communication and persuasion in other cultures she has researched.[11] I have come to rely on findings like those of Meyer's when advising professionals in other parts of the world.

Women Are in an Accelerated Revolution

One of the criticisms I've faced over the years is that I'm not aggressive enough or assertive enough, or maybe somehow, because I'm empathetic, it means I'm weak. I totally rebel against that. I refuse to believe that you cannot be both compassionate and strong.

— Jacinda Ardern, *Former Prime Minister of New Zealand*

We cannot simply talk away the inequities. But I do know this: Language is power. The things we say out loud become real simply by saying them.

Lamenting our powerlessness and allowing others to mistakenly underscore powerless communication as something to aspire to will only enable the barriers. If we continue to insist women are not as credible as men, we will create that expectation. Are those patterns interruptible? Yes. We don't need to bemoan the inequities. Instead, let's *become* the equities.

But where does the castigation need to end? If we continue to insist that "women are harder on women," we will act that way. If we react to strong women by labeling them as "aggressive," we will continue to advance the stereotype that boldness in women is aggressiveness. If we stay silent when others label them that way, we are just as culpable. Assertiveness is not aggressiveness, and it comes in many shapes and sizes. It *should* look different on each of us. Let's applaud that strength.

Speaking powerfully will accelerate our influence, and this book is full of stories of triumph. If you think about the most persuasive women you've encountered, they've likely decided to speak powerfully. If you're one of them, good for you.

The most effective female persuaders are likely personifying the established research that a *combination* of competence and warmth is the most credible leadership style for women. (By the way, research finds this combination is the most effective for men as well.) In fact, recent exciting research has found that companies led by women are more profitable.[12] This just may have something to do with the fact that women executives are reported to lead with more warmth than their male counterparts.

But *deciding* to speak powerfully is not enough. Doing so effectively requires specific approaches, organization, and delivery techniques wrapped in an authentic package. Here we go.

The Six Explosive Steps of Kind Dynamite

Here are the six exciting steps we women can take to use our explosive and compassionate power to influence others:

1. *Create instant credibility* in the first 15 seconds of your message by making your listener curious (Chapter 2).
2. Ensure your listener *keeps* listening to your remarks by overcoming nervousness and using impromptu structures that *stick* (Chapters 3 and 4).
3. Capitalize on the *12 specific strengths* we women have in our voice and nonverbal communication (Chapter 5).
4. Increase the ways you can pull colleagues *toward action* rather than burning time with vagueness (Chapter 6).
5. Take on persuasiveness with those who are *polarized* in their attitudes (Chapter 7).
6. Tailor the way you approach important conversations with the two *most difficult personalities* we encounter in the professional setting (Chapter 8).

And for two bonus steps, I will introduce you to the most effective ways to persuade with PowerPoint and the different ways to show up when you're in an online meeting (Chapters 9 and 10).

CHAPTER 2

Step One: Raise Their Curiosity

Persuasion happens through the unexpected.

I t's 1993, and I'm sitting in a conference room of a high-powered law firm. Beautiful artwork adorns the walls. A long, walnut table, polished to such a deep shine I don't want to touch it, dominates the room and is flanked by high-backed leather chairs.

I'm the first to arrive, so I wait nervously, my palms creating moist impressions on the high-gloss table before I pull them back into my lap. The smell of fresh gourmet coffee wafts up from the coffee maker stationed on the sideboard, permeating the room with temptation, but I'm too anxious to pour myself a cup.

Ten minutes after the meeting was scheduled to begin, the door finally opens.

Here goes, Lisko, I think. *It's time to impress.*

But instead of the expected entourage of incoming trial lawyers, in walks a solitary man dressed in a ragged sweatshirt and baggy jeans.

I exhale slightly at this false start, surmising he is here to service the room. He silently walks toward the front of the room, but instead of checking the state of the coffee I've been too nervous to touch, he takes a seat at the head of the table.

Before I can express my confusion, the door opens again, and in walks the entourage of suits I'd been expecting. As they take their seats around the man in the sweatshirt and look toward him, a wave of realization hits me. The man in the sweatshirt is Lead Counsel, whom I have only met by phone to this point (it's the 1990s, after all — a time before the internet could educate me on his appearance).

He's the epicenter of the trial team suing Exxon Corporation over deep losses Alaskans experienced when the oil tanker, The Exxon Valdez, hit a reef off the coast of Alaska, spilling hundreds of millions of gallons of oil into the water and along the shoreline of Prince William Sound, devastating wildlife and the vital economy of the fishing industry and other native Alaskans for untold years to come.

I'm in this opulent conference room at the invitation of the Lead Counsel and the trial team he leads. I represent the jury research arm of the trial consulting firm they've hired to administer community surveys and run mock trials to gauge what jury-eligible Alaskans think of our case.

My job is to advise the trial team about strategies that will appeal to these jurors.

I set my notes at right angles to the table's edge, as if their perpendicular nature will straighten my jagged nerves. Skipping the welcoming niceties, Lead Counsel finally trains his eyes on me and says, "Well?"

Now, let me pause the story right there (for dramatic effect, of course). Here I am, a 28-year-old woman, one year out from completing my doctoral program at The University of Kansas, but emboldened by my mentor and boss, Joyce Tsongas, who believed in my smarts and in my research about jury decision-making so much that she'd sent me from our jury consulting office in Portland, Oregon, to this conference room in this law firm in Minneapolis.

I had so much to tell the team and an equal measure of nerves to match. And yet, despite that knowledge, I questioned my right to have a seat at the table. Surely, this team of experienced attorneys knew everything I was about to say before I said it.

I clear my throat, stand, straighten the skirt of the pale pink suit I'd proudly purchased with one of my first paychecks, and say, "Well, you know, I'm pretty sure we have learned some things —"

A suit among the many seated around the table cuts in. "Pretty sure? We just paid you a lot of money to conduct jury research, and you're only pretty sure?"

In that moment, I lose my place.

Worse, I lose the floor.

Suit after suit chimes in with theories of what the jury needs most. Five billion dollars is at stake if we win. If the jury goes our way, it will be the largest verdict in American history. I sit back down, fuming at them for taking over and even madder at myself for letting them.

Why tell you this story in a chapter titled *Step One: Raise Their Curiosity*? Because a good story is one of the most powerful ways to get your audience to lean in from the start. It certainly works from the podium, but it isn't always realistic to have this much square footage in a meeting.

My experience in this conference room also highlights something I'm going to teach you how to avoid — something I call a first-line miss. *If only* I'd started my comment in the Exxon meeting by making a Curiosity Filter™ statement. If I'd done so, I guarantee you I would have gotten their attention and respect within the first 10 seconds. I would also have been proud of my verbal power.

I know this because ever since I intentionally began using Curiosity Filter statements, I have drawn far more powerful and focused reactions from my listeners. I have coached a great many professionals to do the same, and they, too, have witnessed that same about-face from their listeners.

What the Curiosity Filter Is Not

Think about the last several meetings you attended. Can you recall attention-getting lines out of *any* of the statements that *anyone* made? It's unlikely.

If you do recall any, it's likely they stand out because they rarely happen. In the lion's share of meetings I attend, participants start the conversation with trite statements like:

"I have something to say."
"Can I make a comment?"
"Let me interject."

It's not just that these first sentences are boring and mind-numbingly unpersuasive. It's worse than that. Thin-slice research finds that people can make startlingly accurate judgments about a speaker's credibility based on only 10 to 30 seconds of information.[13]

So, why on earth do we burn so much time making remarks filled with preamble like, "Hey, how's everyone doing today? So glad you're here. Let's get started." I've been guilty of wasting these precious moments myself. The culprit is simply *not thinking ahead* about starting with something more interesting.

Women often complain that they get interrupted more than men or that they say things in meetings that a man might then paraphrase and be awarded origination credit for the woman's remark. To keep this from happening, you must say *something* to stand out, break that pattern, grab the floor, and hold it.

Enter the Curiosity Filter.

Why the Curiosity Filter Is Fire

"I'm not okay."

Maria Shriver, journalist and former First Lady of California, delivered this first line at the California Women's Conference more than 15 years ago. I was in the audience, and the power of that first sentence has stayed with me ever since.

No boring preamble. No niceties about the weather. Just raw candor. In the sellout crowd of thousands of women and men, everyone leaned forward with anticipation to hear Maria's second sentence. Three words (well, four, if you dissect the contraction) put us on the edge of our seats. "I'm not okay" launched her poignant speech about her grief journey over the loss of her mother months earlier. She made us curious, and she filtered the remainder of her remarks through that powerful first sentence.

Over the years, I've taught others to capitalize on the power of their first sentence and seen it done with such impact that this entire chapter is dedicated to your first sentence.

Now, you might be thinking, *Well, sure. That's fine for someone who had time to ponder her first line for a speech. But comments in meetings are far more impromptu.* That very fact is the reason why using the Curiosity Filter in meetings gains you *even more* credibility. So few people think about their first sentence when making a comment that you will *immediately* stand out when you take a few beats to create one.

As I mentioned before, women professionals often tell me they are interrupted more often than their male colleagues. Some also lament the experience of making a comment, feeling ignored, and watching a second person make a similar comment only to get credit for it.

Both experiences are real, but you have the power to mitigate them. Use your frustration to put energy into starting your comment with a sentence that makes your colleagues curious to hear your next sentence. Doing so will decrease the number of times you're interrupted.

Let's get into the details. There are four types of Curiosity Filters that will work beautifully depending on your objective:

1. The Originating Filter
2. The Quote Filter
3. The Bridge Filter
4. The Enumerator-Plus Filter

Across all four, two facts stand out: First, creating Curiosity Filters requires mindfulness. And second, the more you use them, the easier (and more fun) using them will become.

Curiosity Filter #1: The Originating Filter

When you prepare a comment in a meeting unattached to any comments made before yours, you have the freedom to start with something novel and attention-getting. These qualities have impact because:

- A strong Curiosity Filter is quotable.
- A strong Curiosity Filter is often cryptic.

Remember the Exxon Valdez opening remark that I blew so many years ago? I would have made a far stronger case for myself if I'd instead started my presentation by saying, "The millions of gallons of oil spilled at Prince William Sound *cannot* be the main character in your story."

Does that statement make you curious about who I think the main character should be? It should. *That* is the beauty of this simple but powerful concept.

All it took was a little forethought about how I could start in a cryptic, quotable way that would immediately signal that my comments were going to stand out. There's also power in starting with a counterintuitive statement. The tragic effects of the pollution from the spilled oil could not be understated. It was also intuitive to many on the trial team to make the pollution the focus of their argument, and I was about to advise them away from that intuition.

Remember this chapter's opening quote: *Persuasion happens through the unexpected.* I say it a lot. It's true for audiences of all types, including juries. Had we put too much emphasis on the spillage, the story would have mattered but it would not have had as much impact on the jury. Our mock-trial research told us a different main character *had to be* our emphasis. (If you're still curious, in Chapter 3, I'll tell you who the main character needed to be.)

Curiosity Filter #2: The Quote Filter

I'm most excited to introduce you to the Quote Filter. I use this one the most in meetings, and it always raises curiosity *as long as* I don't rush the delivery. If you're a woman who has ever felt sheepish about raising a good idea in a meeting, *use this filter.* It will make you stand out in a novel way.

What do I mean? A strong Curiosity Filter statement means you must not use a preamble like, "Here's a thought," *and* you must not rush to the second sentence. Allow a pause after you deliver your opening sentence. The pause may feel protracted to you, but it will not feel that way to your listener. Honor their need to absorb what you just said.

The big advantage of the Quote Filter is the way it sets up your subsequent sentences. I will cover the technique for most effectively organizing your subsequent sentences in Chapter 3.

The architecture of a Quote Filter *always* includes something people have heard before, coupled with an unexpected twist. Consider:

- "Have a seat and make yourself uncomfortable." I use this Curiosity Filter statement to tell my listeners that assertiveness often comes with creating and feeling discomfort.
- "If you don't have anything nice to say, think of a better way to say it." This familiar quote twists the listener's expectations to underscore the speaker's right to say even the unpleasant things.

The architecture of a Quote Filter also *frequently* uses an unfamiliar quote from a familiar source, such as:

- Jazz musician Miles Davis said, "When you hit a wrong note, it's the next note that makes it good or bad." I use this Quote Filter statement when talking about owning a mistake and making the next move better because of it.

The architecture of a Quote Filter *sometimes* involves rearranging the furniture of a quote to make it novel. Here are some examples:

- Convert "Life is what happens when we are busy making plans" to "Plans don't always need to happen when we are busy living life."
- Convert "Do one thing every day that scares you" to "Scare one thing away every day by doing it."
- Convert "Imitation is the sincerest form of flattery" to "Hollow flattery is the most insincere form of imitation."

This approach is likely to draw quizzical looks. *That is the intent.* Now you have the full attention of everyone in the room and you can move on to your next sentence.

If you're going to use a Quote Filter to say something quotable you've come up with, the architecture should *always* include your personal philosophies of life. Nothing will come more easily to you than your own way of thinking.

For example, my sweet, brilliant (and sometimes maddening) husband and I adamantly live by our own quotable commitment that "The secret to happiness as we age is to expand our world, not shrink it." And when I speak to audiences about how to deliver a "helpful no" to a client, I start by saying, "Be a window and not a door."

Curious about that?

See? It worked.

Quotes you create yourself can *frequently* take the form of analogies tailored to your setting. For example, consider a discussion about my project manager's responsibilities.

Suppose I start the meeting conversation by saying, "Asking our project manager to also be in charge of our program materials is like asking a commercial jet mechanic to create the airline's marketing brochures."

Notably, this is my first line. It is *not* my third line watered down by the more predictable, "I want to talk about the added burden we are putting on our talented project manager. Here's what I'm thinking…" If I make that mistake, my naysayers have already shut down to my comments, dooming my analogy to failure.

Once you start using this amazing tool, you will become addicted. Just remember not to make the mistake of recycling the same quotes with the same team, or your persuasive impact will dim. We have all encountered "that guy" before — the one who has the same small repertoire of sayings that become trite with time.

The remedy? Continually harvest new quotes — either those you find or those you create yourself. The good news is that becoming a "quote collector" is simple. When I hear a clever turn of phrase or see one come across my day (or across my mind), I write it down or record it on my phone.

To house your growing array of quotes, you'll want to choose a medium that you can access in a meeting. Is it a journal? Is it your phone or laptop? Your quote collection must be readily available to you to be of any use.

Curiosity Filter #3: The Bridge Filter

Since meetings are about dialogue, not monologue, an ideal Curiosity Filter is one that bridges from what your colleague just said to what you want to say next. Of course, there are plenty of boring ways to bridge that do little to set your credibility apart, such as:

- "I agree with what Harry just said."
- "I sort of disagree."
- "That won't work."

None of these examples are distinctive ways to begin. The rubber-stamp "I agree" or flat-out negative is so common that it could invite interruption before you complete your point.

Have you ever found yourself impatiently waiting for someone to complete their remark in a meeting simply so you can weigh in? Or have you become an interrupter? If you said you've never done that, think again. Think about what you would accomplish if you reflected on what was said and came up with a bridge to connect your point in a novel, floor-grabbing way. What if it looked something like this: "What Harry just said, I see as 80 percent true and 20 percent false."

Now you can note where you agree with what everyone in the room just heard, *and* your listeners will want to know where you're headed with your "20 percent false" claim. Your listeners will lean in to hear the rest (more on this in Chapter 3).

Curiosity Filter #4: The Enumerator-Plus Filter

In a pinch, you might not have a quotable phrase at the ready. You can still create a Curiosity Filter if you *enumerate* with some added creative punch. We all know the power of enumeration, but there is a way to add curiosity through creativity.

This is the never-fail filter in that enumerating always works to grab attention. However, be careful not to over-use it. If you earn the title of The Enumerator among your colleagues, you have clearly gone too far.

Though Enumerator-Plus Filters use numbers to make a point, they go a level deeper. While starting with something like, "I have two thoughts about that," should minimize interruptions, this approach doesn't build much curiosity.

Instead, consider these next-level approaches that will make your listener take notice of what you've said:

- "Two things are true, and one is false."
- "We may have thought all along there was one solution to this problem when it turns out there are three."

My use of the number three in that last example was a cheat, and here's why. Recently, I was coaching a wonderful client and recommended this Enumerator-Plus Filter approach. She countered, "Karen, my brain doesn't work that way. What do I do about the fact that my brain always adds another item to the list mid-sentence?"

I lit up. "That regularly happens to me too!" I said.

The solution is to *always add one* when you deliver your Enumerator-Plus Filter. If I can readily think of two items, I say there are three. Invariably, I think of a third by the time I complete my second item. In those exceptionally rare circumstances when I don't think of a third, I use humor to tell my listeners that it turned out my three items could be economized into two or perhaps that the third thought was reserved for them to contribute!

Prepare for the Pause

Think of the delivery of your Curiosity Filter as akin to delivering a "one-liner." It may be the verbal foot you put in the door of a lively conversation. It may be the first comment anyone has made in a few beats. Either way, build in a few seconds of pause. This act requires you to overcome your own discomfort with silence, and then it sets you well to deliver the body of your remarks.

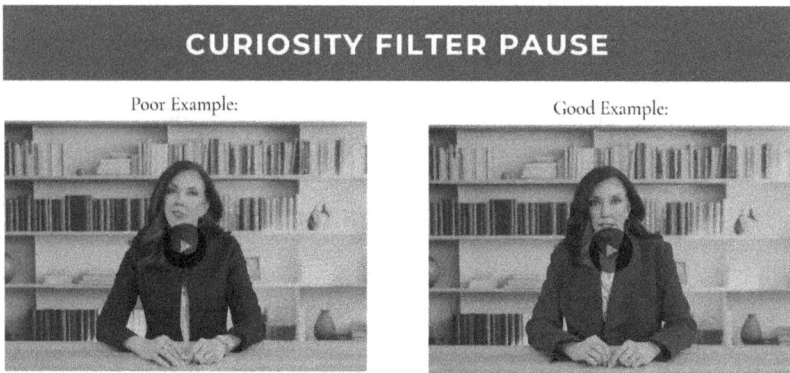

CURIOSITY FILTER PAUSE

Poor Example:

Good Example:

Take a look at the difference between an ineffective way to use a Curiosity Filter pause and a more effective way by clicking on the QR code below this image or visiting karenlisko.com/videos.

CHAPTER 3

Step Two: Grab an Other-Centered Mindset

Forget the pressure of being interesting. You'll accomplish so much more by being interested in your audience.

Have you ever started a conversation by saying, "Off the top of my head"? A lead-in like that is an indicator of disorganized remarks that rarely help your credibility. In fact, if you think about the number of meetings you've attended in your professional lifetime, I'd bet you've heard many more disorganized comments than organized ones. I'd also bet those comments were not memorable.

And again, as a woman, you may have made a comment, felt ignored, and then watched someone else make a similar comment and get the credit. It isn't always a gender thing. Could it have been your (dis)organization? I'll raise my hand to admit to rambling in a meeting. Who hasn't? The content that follows this top-of-mind comment is typically true to its word — disorganized and often unclear.

If you listen to interviews conducted on podcasts or on the radio, you may have encountered well-known writers or print media reporters who seemed surprisingly meandering in that environment. I have a theory about that. Terrific writers have time to hone their words and organize their thoughts when the cursor on their laptop is blinking at them. But they — like most of the rest of us — don't always treat verbal, impromptu remarks as something that needs to be so structured. And yet, without structure, they sound disorganized.

Scripting Yourself Is Not the Solution

To guard against a disorganized presentation, many professionals create a script. However, this creates other problems.

Several weeks ago, a highly accomplished attorney in her 50s named Brinna asked me to coach her to become more effective in her "meeting speak." When I met her face-to-face for the first time in my office in Seattle, not only was the sunny day pulling out the blue in the Puget Sound a stark contrast to Seattle's recent cloudy grayness, but Brinna's friendly demeanor when talking casually contrasted with her rehearsed meeting remarks.

Here's how things unfolded.

We sat across from one another in a conference room on the 49th floor. I offered Brinna coffee, and she joked about taking it intravenously for greater impact. Brinna was bright, funny, and well-spoken when we were in the small-talk phase of our appointment. Then we started to workshop her meeting style. I asked Brinna to demonstrate how she typically launches into a key meeting topic, and an entirely different version of her appeared.

She became so monotone and formal that I had to lean in to check the blurring of her earlier dynamism. I interrupted, asking why a different version of her had appeared.

She took a beat, then responded, "I'm trying to sound professional." Before I could interject, she admitted she was also more nervous in that mode and was concerned she would forget something important she had to say. As a result, she was relying on handwritten notes in front of her. Had Brinna stayed in her more conversational style, she would have sounded so much more confident and persuasive! Instead, she'd been telling herself for years to show up a different way in meetings, and it was holding her back.

Brinna was like so many professionals who have been coaching themselves into a more formal, less-effective mode simply because they have seen so many others before them adopt the same style.

Avoid the Vicious Script Cycle

If you fear forgetting an important point, you're in good company. Anecdotally, I find women are more concerned about this possibility (or at least, they are more willing to admit it). I routinely find that the more nervous speakers I coach are often the same people who write out their remarks word-for-word, specifically to ensure they sound more organized and to protect against dropping an important point. But this creates the problem that I call the "Vicious Script Cycle."

Image 1: *The Vicious Script Cycle*

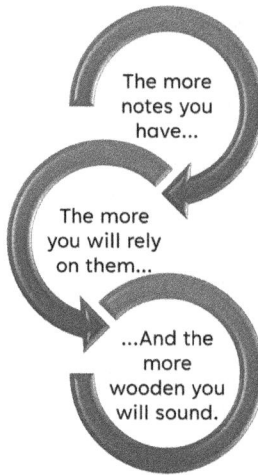

The more notes you have...

The more you will rely on them...

...And the more wooden you will sound.

The more notes you have, the more you will rely on them. And the more you rely on them, the more wooden you will sound. So, your attempt to sound more organized actually sounds more nervous and low energy.

Professional and Personable: A Nonnegotiable Combination

Like Brinna, too many female professionals believe they must choose between being professional *or* personable. To that, I say, forget that "fool's choice," as conversational researchers put it.

Communication research consistently finds that the most credible female speakers in meetings or at the podium are *both* professional and personable. And if you're reluctant to believe the research, trust your own experience. Think of the last few female colleagues you've seen speak up beautifully and persuasively in a meeting. Ask yourself, were they *only* professional? Were they *only* personable? Or were they both?

I guarantee they were both. Whether that ability came to them naturally or through their own self-realization that they should exhibit the combination of Kind (personable and warm) Dynamite (professional and competent), it works. And these women know it. Believe that about your own potential and give yourself permission to show up as both personable *and* professional. You can absolutely do this.

We often mistakenly think impromptu remarks inherently lack structure. That simply isn't true. Well-delivered impromptu remarks that follow your Curiosity Filter statement can propel your message in a way that makes them stand out. The secret here is to apply simple structures that most others won't — and you'll be noticed for it.

When working with Brinna, I first needed to change her mind about this crucial combination of professionalism and personality to start growing her credibility in meetings. Then, we got to work developing organizational techniques and adding persuasive delivery.

As I explained to Brinna, powerful impromptu remarks require three key elements:

1. An other-centered mindset to boost your confidence.
2. Other-centered language that incorporates your audience.
3. A structure that keeps your listener's attention and makes a *completely clear point.*

In this chapter, I'll discuss the first two, and then I'll cover the third element in Chapter 4.

Element #1: Adopt an Other-Centered Mindset

I've had the privilege of coaching countless confident women and men. Most of them have postgraduate degrees in law, medicine, or business. They've spoken up in a lot of meetings and routinely address the C-suite in their company or have spoken as members of the C-suite themselves. Despite that mileage in meetings, *virtually all* of them confess to feeling some nerves when speaking up in key meetings. For some, their nervousness is significant. Their peers may not see it, but it's there. The trick to their success is that many of them have figured out how to get out of their own "self-centered self-talk."

They have found their way to *other-centered* speaking, where they make the listener the focus of the remark rather than making themselves the central character in their comments. *This* is Kind Dynamite. An other-centered mindset enables us to focus on our goals instead of ourselves or our fears of how others will see us.

In her book, *The Greatness Game*, Greatness Coach Dena Patton (how cool is that job title?) begins by saying, "The power to believe and agree with your greatness is already within you. It is a choice to come out of agreement with your smallness."[14]

I most definitely remember feeling small in meetings. Remember the Exxon Valdez trial team meeting I described? After that experience, I knew I had to accelerate showing up in a way that instilled confidence in my messaging, or I would end up in yet another conference room frustrated with losing the floor. I had to get out of my own smallness for the sake of my clients and for myself. We both deserved that. And more to the point, my clients were paying me for my confidence in my messaging. I was there to help them achieve their goals. My worries about myself were in the way.

Have you ever felt that smallness within? Think about the confident women (and men) you encounter in meetings. Those who knock it out of the park using the combination of compassion and competence that are the hallmark of Kind Dynamite seem to have figured out how to move out of their smallness.

If you want to speak with Kind Dynamite, there are three techniques I recommend that will help you take an other-centered role when your nerves compete with your good intentions.

Technique #1: Pretend You're a Dinner Host

Hear me out. Of course, you're not *actually* hosting a dinner during the meeting. Sadly, there may be no food there at all. But try this exercise: Think about the last time you hosted someone in your home for dinner. Now, think about the last time you were a guest in someone else's home. Did you behave differently when you were the host compared to when you were the guest? Most of us do.

When we host others, we're typically more outgoing, more dynamic, and more other-centered (that is, after we've rushed around cleaning house!). Use that exact energy in a meeting, even if you're not the meeting host and even when you're more junior to others in the meeting.

At a minimum, you're the host of your *remarks*. You may have thought more about your remarks than someone senior to you. Do *not* wait to be called on, and do *not* wait to be the more senior person in the room to contribute your smart comment. I repeatedly urge clients to adopt this mindset, and this shift alone pulls out a Kind Dynamite demeanor in most.

And one significant bonus? You may just find you have less time to feel nervous. Get lost in your focus on others, and your self-focus will fade away.

The other reason this dinner-host mindset works so well is because it reflects an "authentic you" in your more outgoing role. Just like you must compartmentalize dinner-party worries (*Did I make enough food? Did I remember to refill the soap dispenser in the powder room?*) while being genuinely focused on taking care of your guests, you likely need to compartmentalize internal business-meeting worries (*What if they think my idea is too basic? What if I'm wrong?*). The challenge is to do this while putting your colleagues at ease with you around the conference table or around the virtual meeting room.

It is *not disingenuous* to compartmentalize; it is often downright essential. You are not being fake; you're mentally multi-tasking.

And here's a reality check. If you wait to feel that your internal worries are quelled enough to share your thoughts, that time may never come. Even worse, someone else may have voiced your good idea aloud while you were silently dialoguing with your internal worries. Get that unneces-sary noise out of your head. Trust yourself.

Technique #2: Focus on Your Audience During Your Travel Time

If you're driving to an important in-person meeting (or walking several steps to your home office for a virtual one), use that travel time wisely by focusing on your audience rather than on yourself.

I didn't always know this trick. I used to spend my drive time absorbed in the remarks I was going to make, worrying about delivering my talking points in the right order, and getting even more panicked I would forget something important. And then, one day, I just...stopped.

I realized I was using my travel time to be self-centered about my remarks when what made so much more sense was to focus my travel thoughts on what I hoped to do for my listeners. Where would my comments help them? Where did I hope to help them grow? That simple shift in focus decreased my own nervousness and made me feel excited about making my upcoming remarks. I was the teacher.

Technique #3: Filter Your Listening Through Curiosity

This Curiosity Filter concept has so many lives!

When was the last time you listened — truly and com-pletely listened — to your colleague's comments without impatience and without judgment? It isn't that easy unless you consciously assign yourself the task.

Intelligent brains can feel like hyperactive ones simply because we *can* carry multiple thoughts (and have internal conversations with ourselves) at the same time. That ability crowds our capacity to be singularly focused on the person speaking.

And don't get me started on our perverse tendency to often tune out the speaker when we think they're saying the same thing they always do. Maybe they are. In that case, jolt yourself out of thinking the same thing you always think and push yourself to respond differently. If they *aren't* saying the same thing they always do, your "pre-listening" has too hastily shut down your ability to fully hear with fresh ears.

Be freshly curious. Treat the other person's comments like interesting data, even if you disagree. Mine for opportunities to go in *without* preplanned remarks on frequent occasions. Instead, listen for a cue to use a Bridge Filter that quotes your colleague and then moves to your point. How, exactly? Read on.

Element #2: Use Other-Centered Language

Other-centered remarks do more than calm your nerves or make you look forward to making a powerful comment. This other-centered approach also changes your listener. And, in my experience, we women are wired to have this superpower more readily than the men.

Neuroscience research has *exponentially exploded* our understanding of the brain and persuasion in recent years, including helping us understand the parts of the brain that "light up" when we make decisions. As persuaders, knowing some of these key findings is gold. What excites me is the fact that a Kind Dynamite approach to speaking helps drive the decisions we want our listener to make.

For most of us, we process information through the emotional part of our brain *first* and through our logical center *second*. Some of us dwell for longer periods of time in one part of our brain and some of us bounce around, but the *beginnings* of our information processing are typically emotional.

Think about your last major purchase — a laptop, a car, a home. If our brains were studied using functional magnetic resonance imaging (fMRI), neuroscientists would more frequently see our emotional center light up *first* as we process what we want, what draws us to one item over the other, and even what emotionally ties us to the inanimate object of our desire. *Then*, we move to our logical center to intellectually justify the purchase. The better laptop will make us work faster; the nicer car is safer; the more expensive home is a better investment.

Our intellectual justifications aren't wrong, but the emotional drive toward the item is also real. Still, some in your sphere will tell you they make all decisions unemotionally. Neuroscience would say they are kidding themselves. They may *feel* unemotional, but their emotional center likely played some role in breaking a tie between — or incorporating both — wants and needs.

Why It Works: Taking a Cue from Litigation Research

So, what does this neuroscience lesson have to do with other-centered remarks? The answer is at once both simple and complex. When the listener is the focus of your remarks, you appeal to their emotions. That's the simple part. Determining *how* to appeal to their priorities is often more difficult.

A major part of my job as a social scientist in litigation persuasion is to understand what appeals to juries, judges, and arbitrators. Over the past three decades, I have certainly seen patterns of what matters to them, including the fact that all fact-finders are humans whose emotions intertwine with their logic. But I will also humbly say that I'm still often surprised as hell at what matters to a fact-finder in a specific case. That is why clients spend many thousands of dollars to have us run mock trials to determine how emotions and logic play in fact-finders' views of the evidence for a specific case.

Once the research is done, we focus on putting the fact finder's emotional priorities into our persuasive appeals. For example:

What might seem like a boring *breach of contract* case is really...	➡	a story of excited optimism between two parties that ended in disheartening rubble.
What feels like a technically dense *patent dispute* is really...	➡	a drama about an inventor's deep wish to improve the world only to find that her invention had already been patented by someone else.

In both examples, a "pure logic" approach would have focused myopically on contract language or disproportionately on patented claim terminology. And neither would have reached the emotional center of the fact finder.

How to Pull Other-Centeredness into Your Meeting Remarks

There are cool ways you can pull on your colleagues' emotional centers without seeming over the top. You know you've accomplished an other-centered appeal with your peers if you conduct a "language inventory" and find you're being other-centered.

Language Inventory Item 1	Are you making your colleagues your central character? Inventory how often you talk about yourself versus how often you make your colleagues in front of you the main characters in your examples.
Language Inventory Item 2	Are you capitalizing on the most important word you should use? The simple act of maximizing the number of times you use the pronoun "you" and minimizing the pronoun "I" will transform how other-centered you sound to your listener. The next time you make a comment in a meeting, count your pronouns.
Language Inventory Item 3	Are you speaking in the singular voice? When you address a group of people, they understandably look plural to you. But they *don't* feel plural to themselves. Talk to them in the singular voice to avoid making them feel that you see them as a group. Instead of saying, "Some of you," say "you" in the singular.

CHAPTER 4

Step Two, Continued: Use Impromptu Structures that Impress

N ow it's time to address the third key element of a strong and memorable impromptu remark: structure. The beauty of a well-structured impromptu remark is that it exponentially boosts your credibility. Why? Because so few speakers put thought into using even the simplest structures. Even fewer keep practicing the techniques once they learn them. Use your superpower as a woman to be tenacious!

If you adopt an effective structure, you will stand out among your meeting colleagues. And to be clear about the definition of *impromptu*, consider the reality that most remarks we make in meetings come with a minute or two of forethought. While someone else wraps up their re-mark, your smart brain can listen (to some degree) while you also note a few structured thoughts in your mind or in your notes.

If you try one or more of the approaches I'm about to teach you, I promise you two things will occur:

1. **You will be initially annoyed with the clunkiness of a structured approach.** Importing a structure where you have not used one will feel awkward and forced — that is until you have some practice. Then, you will find using a structure comes naturally. But make no mistake. Practicing these impromptu structures takes repeated, conscious effort at first. If you commit to getting past that "clunkiness," you will stand out. If you put these ideas away on a shelf, your persuasiveness will sit on the shelf with them.

2. **You will love the clarity with which you deliver your message.** You won't be alone. Your listener will understand your point more clearly and re-member your argument better. You will also be in-terrupted less!

Create a Two-Part Structure Using Quotables

A good quote can clatter around in our brains for de-cades. For example, at the time I'm writing this book, it's been 30 years since the criminal trial of accused murderer OJ Simpson when his defense counsel said in their closing argument, "If the glove doesn't fit, you must acquit." Today, audiences of varying ages still immediately recognize that quote.

Building upon my prior discussion of quotes as a device, consider creating a quote bank of your favorites to have handy for a meeting. If you're fortunate enough to meet with different listeners in your work, you can always recycle your favorites — a strategy I routinely use. To take these quotes to the next level, use them as a structural home for your comments. Look at how you can take these two-parters out for a spin:

- **"Your point is both right and wrong.** Where you're right is that we do need to move forward with our growth plan in this market. Where you're wrong is that the more urgent market for this growth plan is one we haven't yet discussed."

- **"Nothing ventured, nothing gained.** We were too risk-averse to take a chance on this product and, as a result, we have gained nothing. In fact, we're standing still while the competition is moving ahead."

- **"More than one thing can be true, and in this case, that's exactly where we are.** The first truth is that we need to develop pro bono projects with our clients. The second truth is that developing our pro bono efforts for the client benefits our staff at the same time."

The more you use quotables to start your statements, the more memorable your remarks will become. Don't be surprised if a colleague compliments you on something that sticks in their mind from this practice. You will also be taken more seriously in the process.

How to Tell a Good Story When a Fuller Message Is Possible

While you don't always have the "impromptu luxury" to tell a full story, sometimes that option exists. And if you do have the option to tell a story, you don't want to waste your time on a me-andering structure. If you're short on time or need to keep your remarks brief, you must focus on using shorter micro-stories.

The power of the story is not simply that people like a well-told one. The superpower of the story is that it wins out over general commentary every single time. In fact, impres-sive research that synthesized 75 studies testing story and memory involving a total of 33,000 subjects found that story is more memorable for the listener.[15] *That* is story's super-power. If the story is memorable, so are you as the storyteller.

You have been listening to (and probably telling) stories your entire life. I suspect you've been subjected to badly told ones and have also been treated to brilliantly told ones. What creates the divide between the bad and the brilliant?

Disney-Pixar's Never-Fail Story Structure

There's an open secret about the structure of a well-told story that Disney and Pixar have formulaically used for decades. Let's follow the story of Cinderella to examine the four fundamental steps of a well-told story, and then we'll look at how you might apply these steps to tell a brilliant micro-story in a meeting.

Step One: Normal	Cinderella lives with her evil stepmother and stepsisters, along with very talented mice who keep her company when her stepfamily ignores her. Her situation isn't ideal, but she seems generally happy. She sure sings a lot.
Step Two: Crisis	Cinderella learns of a royal ball where the prince is looking for a bride, and she yearns to go. Her step-monster family locks her in the attic to keep her from going.
Step Three: Intervention	A fairy godmother appears, frees Cinderella, and outfits her for the ball using some very creative magic. Cinderella meets the prince, runs away from her love for him, and clumsily loses her shoe.
Step Four: New Normal	The prince becomes obsessed with her lost shoe, finds her, and they live happily ever after.[16]

Cinderella's story could take a while to tell (the animated version produced by Walt Disney in 1950 lasted 75 minutes), so when it comes to meetings, is it even realistic to run through these four steps in a few minutes or less?

Try this on for size. Assume your goal is to explain to your team that extraordinary customer service is the expectation, *not* the exception, and you want to use the micro-story structure to make your argument memorable.

Step One: Normal	"We had a large client who enjoyed a good reputation with consumers and the public."
Step Two: Crisis	"Then, one of the executives was caught on video while in a heated argument with a subordinate. The video was posted on social media and only showed part of the argument, making the executive look outrageous. The video went viral, and comments quickly accumulated with conclusions about what must be a toxic work environment. The company reached out in a panic about how to handle the situation."
Step Three: Intervention	"Within mere hours, we obtained legal advice on messaging and paired it with a press release and social media posts that emphasized the company's desire to say anything but 'No comment.' The messaging simply and fully supported both employees and provided more context for the circumstances to explain how the partial video mistakenly cast doubts on one of the employee's character."
Step Four: New Normal	"The client received generally favorable comments for going beyond the legalistic 'No comment' and for showing empathy to both employees rather than hunkering down in support of the executive. Now, the company emphasizes empathy in its mission statement."

The "above and beyond" client components included responding extra quickly in this "viral crisis" and encouraging a message that was proactive and compassionate rather than defaulting to a self-protective "No comment."

There is so much more to telling a great story that would double the length of this book — and I know the expert to teach it better than I can. To learn more about telling good stories, check out story master Dr. Sally Perkins and her book, *Noble Cause, Noble Story*.[17]

Make Your Story More Memorable with a Zinger

When we think about a story, we naturally tend to think about *chronology*. Certainly, the story I shared about the company with the PR crisis occurred in chronological order. The plot of classic Disney movies occurs in order as well. But what if you messed with the order of the steps slightly to make your point even more memorable? I'm not talking about doing something as complex as those sci-fi films that often have a flashback or travel a parallel universe — this book is about making persuasive points in meetings, after all! You must keep it simple.

If you have a favorite anecdote about family or friends that you tell, think about the high point or, if there is one, a shock point in that story. *Now*, think about pulling that moment out of chronological order and putting it at the end of your story. This can make your story so much more memorable.

Let's say you want to underscore the fact that taking initiative in business doesn't just have to happen top-down from the executive level. Here's a true story to emphasize that point:

Frank Abagnale Jr. was a genius who wanted to skirt the traditional ways of getting the "cool" jobs. He was a thrill seeker and a con artist. He successfully faked being an airline pilot and a physician, acted as a lawyer, and had so many false identities that it took the Federal Bureau of Investigation (FBI) a while to catch him. They eventually succeeded, and Frank ended up behind bars. Oh, and when the FBI caught him, he wasn't even 21 years old yet! So, when you see initiative in your young employees, I want you to do two things. Take their ideas seriously and check their IDs!

Had I told you at the beginning of the story that Frank wasn't yet 21 years old, it would still have been memorable, but it wouldn't have delivered the same "zing" as when I waited until the end to share that crucial detail.

Use Structured Micro-Stories to Amp Up Your Impromptu Remark

The micro-story approach can use several different impromptu structures. It can also put you on par with those who (again, in my anecdotal experience) seem to tell more stories in a conference room setting — men! As an example of how micro-stories work, let's use a story I often tell about one of my longtime clients.

More than twenty years ago, General Counsel of Kimberly-Clark, maker of Kleenex Tissues and Huggies Diapers, asked me to help with an emergency witness prep on a day when I was already booked. I declined. He called back, offering me some added incentives. Again, I declined.

Then I thought more about his offer and countered, expressing a need for a great many diapers. He agreed to my request, and I was able to finagle a change to my prior commitment and meet with the witness.

I've often used this story as an example of the extra lengths to which we all must occasionally go to create mutual client loyalty. Let's start with how I begin the structure of my micro-story when I'm trying to make this point.

Quotable Part 1	"Have you ever considered the possibility that diapers could create client loyalty?" Note that I've started with a Curiosity Filter instead of a watered-down preamble like, "I have something to say."
Pause	Remember to let your words sink in instead of rushing through what you want to say.
Quotable Part 2	"In fact, my diaper story accomplished two lasting win-wins for my client and for me."

Now that I've grabbed my audience's attention, I have two choices for structuring the rest of my impromptu remark.

Micro-Story Structure Option 1: Two-Part Enumeration

Start by announcing that you're going to share a two-part story. You'll spend the first half of your remarks focused on telling the story and the second half sharing your philosophical lesson. With this structure in mind and the goal of illustrating how going the extra mile can build mutual loyalty, I'll share how I would have told my story about my longtime client.

I'd start part one by saying, "This is a story in two parts. Here's part one: Years ago, General Counsel for Kimberly-Clark, the maker of Huggies Diapers and Kleenex Tissues, asked me to come to Dallas at the last minute to help prepare a witness to testify at trial. I declined because I had a meeting scheduled for the same day. He responded by offering to either send the company jet for me or pay me double my hourly rate. After some finagling, I was able to move my meeting to help the trial witness, but I declined the two incentives he'd offered."

For the second part of my two-part enumeration, I'd say, "What do I mean by that? I only agreed to rearrange my schedule and go to Dallas with such short notice by asking General Counsel for a very different favor in return. My husband and I were in the middle of adopting our third child from an orphanage in Belarus and had just learned that their one-hundred-baby institution had been without diapers *for a year*. I asked General Counsel if he could do something about that.

"He readily complied, and Kimberly-Clark spent the next several months working through the red tape required to move a truckload of diapers across the Belarusian border. Much to the deep relief of the orphanage workers, Kimberly-Clark finally succeeded.

"My client and I both won and formed mutual loyalty through that experience. He told me that having an opportunity to help those children is one of his fondest memories of our working relationship. I felt the same, and I give Kimberly-Clark credit whenever I can."

I could make a fatal error by letting *only the story* dictate the two-part structure. But if I do that, my structure becomes self-centered and immediately less persuasive. Remember, Kind Dynamite persuades through an other-centered approach. Your story can *support* your structure but should not *become* the structure. Here's what I mean:

A Self-Centered Two-Part Structure	An Other-Centered Two-Part Structure
1. Client wanted **me** to do X. 2. **I** wanted Y.	1. Show **your** client **your** willingness. 2. Do overt good with **your** client's gratitude.

Unfortunately, the self-centered structure buries the lessons of the story for the listener. The other-centered structure makes your listener the central character in your impromptu remark.

Micro-Story Structure Option 2: The Triple W

While I wish I could say all meetings I've attended in my lifetime are riveting, I couldn't come close to saying so with a straight face. As a persuasive communication researcher, I'm always listening to my colleagues' remarks and noting how they do (or do not) structure them in meetings. Over time, it struck me that some made much clearer points than others, and I wanted to figure out why.

I started to notice a pattern. Many of those presenting clear points followed a framework I have come to call the Triple W or the What/Why/Where structure. I'm not sure every speaker was aware they were following this approach, but once I diagnosed it, I couldn't stop seeing it, either because someone was using it so well or because someone had dropped an important component. In the latter instance, it was stunning how doing so made their point far less persuasive.

The What/Why/Where Structure
What is the issue?
Why is it significant?
Where does that leave you / the client / the company?

The Triple W must always address what, why, and where in that specific order. Here's a deeper look at each of these elements:

- ***What* is your up-front, bottom-line point?** It immediately conveys your conclusion or your "ask" to your listener.[18] The power of the *What* as your starting point is two-fold. First, it makes it clear where you stand, and second, it conveys confidence. It sounds definitive, not meandering.

- ***Why* is there significance to your bottom-line point?** Put another way, it answers the internal question, "So, what is the big deal about this point?" When you overtly state the significance of your *What*, you make it both more clear and more persuasive. Marking the significance of your main point is not a new concept. Back in the 1950s and again in the early 2000s, Professor Stephen Toulmin[19] described a model of persuasion that included something he called the "warrant." It is synonymous with the *Why* I'm advocating here. Without it, Toulmin argued the speaker's point was less persuasive and credible.

- ***Where* is your opportunity to be other-centered and, therefore, more persuasive?** The *Where* answers the question, "Where does this leave [fill in the blank]?" The "blank filler" might be your company, your client, or someone else who is important to your point. The *Where* can be aspirational and highlight the good that can come from your *What*, or it can be ominous and point out the bad that can come from your *What*.

Because *Where* is the final part of your Triple W structure, its importance is even more significant. For years, social scientists have debated whether the first thing or the last thing you say is the most important. The reality is that both count. But the Triple W structure leans on more recent research findings that argue the *Where* creates a "peak-end" that lingers in the listener's brain.[20]

Now, let's try using the Triple W structure on the Kimberly-Clark story.

The What/Why/Where Structure	
What is the issue?	"The most important thing we can do in our work is to create grateful clients through whom we can 'do good' with their gratitude." After you make this statement, you can share your micro-story about Kimberly-Clark and the diapers delivered to the Belarusian orphanage.
Why is it significant?	"The reason this matters is that it creates a 'sticky relationship' with the client that stands out in their memory, which is exactly what happened with General Counsel at Kimberly-Clark."
Where does that leave you / the client / the company?	"If we succeed in creating that 'stick,' we will have an advantage over our competition and potentially generate further business with the client the next time they need services like ours."

Taking the Triple W Structure to the Next Level

The What/Why/Where structure is your foundation, but if you have the wherewithal (and forethought) to add more credibility to your story, this structure is more complete in *five* parts. Preceding the *What* is your Curiosity Filter and following your *Where* is a "circular bookend" where you return to your Curiosity Filter but in a more developed manner.

The *Expanded* What/Why/Where Structure	
Curiosity Filter	"If I use the phrase *grateful gratitude*, you might think I just messed with proper grammar. In fact, it's a formula for client success."
What is the issue?	"The most important thing we can do in our work is to create grateful clients through whom we can 'do good' with their gratitude." After you make this statement, you can share your micro-story about Kimberly-Clark and the diapers delivered to the Belarusian orphanage.
Why is it significant?	"The reason this matters is that it creates a 'sticky relationship' with the client that stands out in their memory, which is exactly what happened with General Counsel at Kimberly-Clark."
Where does that leave you / the client / the company?	"If we succeed in creating that 'stick,' we will have an advantage over our competition and potentially generate further business with the client the next time they need services like ours."
Circular Bookend	"So, there you have it. Grateful gratitude — something we should consider adding to the next version of company quotables."

You might want to push back on these structures as truly being an impromptu approach since it appears I put in more forethought than simply a few impromptu minutes. To an extent, you're right. I have told the Kimberly-Clark story before. But the lessons I used it to share, along with the way I chose to divvy up the story, were impromptu.

Because I had the story and the structural options in my back pocket, I was able to position it within my remarks on the fly. Think about the many stories you have lived. To make them truly impromptu, have them within reach on a mobile device, in a meeting journal you carry with you, or, if you're one of the lucky few among us, in your memory bank.

In a meeting, I would have used a legal pad to jot down my two lessons before sharing my thoughts using the two-part enumeration structure. Impromptu doesn't mean you have to be completely notes-free! It just means you have come to your impromptu comment during the meeting rather than in advance of it.

Three Mistakes That Will Discount Your Greatness

It would only be fitting to end this chapter with something memorable, as the peak-end rule dictates we do. Here it is: Far too often, we bury an otherwise brilliant point beneath discounts.

Who doesn't like a good discount? Well, if your goal is to be credible, you shouldn't. Too often, we unintentionally but clearly tell our listener *not* to listen to us by discounting the point into a weaker state. There are three common mistakes where these discounts show up:

Mistake #1: Discounting What You're About to Say Before You Say It

If you've ever started a remark by saying, "I could be wrong, but," or, "This might be a bad idea, but," you just watered down a potentially brilliant point. If you aren't certain about an idea, consider more effective ways to say so. For example, you can always qualify your point by saying, "Let's consider one of two ways to go here." With this approach, you provided options that were more declarative and more credible. *That* is dynamite.

Mistake #2: Discounting What You're Saying as You Speak

If you look back at my language examples in this chapter, you will not come across one *kinda*, *maybe*, or *sorta*. Some of us use these verbal intensifiers so frequently that we don't even notice we're doing it.

Sometimes, we kid ourselves into believing that using these words is more kind to the listener as a way to soften our point. It certainly softens your point, but not in a credible way. You can always soften a blunt point through your tone of voice (more on that in Chapter 6.) Trapping your dynamite point in a kinda-maybe-sorta habit only diminishes your appearance of competence.

Mistake #3: Discounting Your Hard-Won Accomplishments

I will never forget sitting in an audience at a law conference many years ago where two attorneys from Fortune 50 companies were panelists who talked about their experience leading their respective legal groups. The two attorneys happened to be of different genders. Ironically, they also happened to say the same exact sentence several minutes apart when reflecting on their careers. At different points, each of them said, "I got lucky."

When the female attorney said it, the audience didn't react.

When the male attorney said it, he was applauded.

Now, what on earth caused those different reactions? The sentence felt authentically humble coming from both. Both carried equal stature within their corporations. Gender research would tell us the female attorney said it at a time when women had an established reputation for "insulting the compliment" and sounding less confident as a result. The male attorney said it at a time when men had a strong habit of sounding more boastful. As a result, the male attorney's humility drew applause for his self-effacing comment.

Fast forward to today, and we still apply these discounts all too frequently.

Somewhere in our early years, many of us women learned to minimize our accomplishments so beautifully that today it comes back to bite us in the you-know-what. When complimented for our hard-won success on a project, we often kindly say, "It was a team effort" (great), but we fail to say, "I loved getting to be the thought architect on this project," first (not good). Putting both together *is*

Kind Dynamite. Ideally, you should first acknowledge your role and then note your team's solid contributions.

We women need to own our accomplishments with grace and confidence and use Kind Dynamite to ensure that we mentor our colleagues to do the same. It is not arrogant to acknowledge our contributions. It is smart.

Save the discounts for the Nordstrom Half-Yearly Sale.

CHAPTER 5

Step Three: Leave Them Impressed with a Concrete Call to Action

What you say makes things real.
How you say it makes things happen.

If only your comments *during* the meeting signaled the end of your persuasive job. But stopping there is like running a race and then not even trying to cross the finish line. Your job during the meeting is to foretell what action you want to create *after* the meeting. We women have a super-power for follow-through, and this is simply a "messaging extension" of that ability.

To make sure there's follow-through after a meeting, you must first Create Continuing Credibility (the Three C's) that leaves your colleagues or clients impressed and Set Specific Steps (the Three S's) you and your colleagues can put into action. The Three C's and the Three S's are intrinsically linked.

Let's go back to my entrepreneurial friend Becky App, her business partner Abby Jordan, and the hit reality television show *Shark Tank*. Becky and Abby knew they needed to achieve the Three C's to stand out among the other entrepreneurs and to potentially appear in a rerun. As smart businesswomen, they knew the exposure their business received on *Shark Tank* would literally convert to dollars when viewers saw the show and visited their website (and it did). If they could Create Continuing Credibility that earned them a rerun of their televised segment, they could get double the exposure and even more revenue (and they did).

The show's producers knew the show's success depended on showcasing the Three S's. Imagine what might have happened if the producers of the show didn't require Becky and Abby to be specific about their "ask." Imagine what might have happened had the Sharks decided to just "let Becky and Abby know what they might do for them at some later, undefined point" based on not knowing what the eCreamery founders concretely wanted. If that was the case, this long-running show would not have lasted more than a few episodes. Without specificity, there's no decisiveness, no drama, and no closure. You can also predict that very few budding entrepreneurs would ever hear from the

Sharks who promised to try to get back to them "at some point."

Does this scenario sound familiar to you? How many times have you sat in a meeting wondering what the concrete objective was other than to provide updates that could have easily been summarized in an email? Or how many times have you left the meeting with no clear plan of action? Have you ever been guilty of creating this "meeting blur" yourself?

> **Without specificity, there's no decisiveness, no drama, and no closure.**

Let's make it better.

Create Continuing Credibility

Think about the stand-out memories you have of others' credible comments in meetings. There is more than a small chance that those comments stood out for one of the following reasons:

- They spoke in quotables.
- They used tension as a "go-to" rather than a "run-from."
- They made you or someone else feel heard.

Want to Share?

If you have other cool examples you want to share, I would love to hear from you. Simply go to karenlisko.com and post your example. I'll keep your identity anonymous if you wish.

Create Credibility with Self-Citable Quotables

Think back to Chapter 2, when I shared how to use a Curiosity Filter. You'll recall I urged using a Quote Filter and starting a comment with a quote, then repurposing the quote as a comment. My advice to speak in quotables here is different. Use your own smarts to create your own quotables that may simply fit into one of your points (rather than serving as a structural Curiosity Filter).

I gravitate to people who work quotables into their comments. For example, some of the best quotes I have collected over the years came out of the mouths of colleagues — often without their advance planning.

Quote	Context
"We can be cheaper than the competition, or we can be better. We aren't cheaper."	You are explaining your higher rate to a prospective client.
"Assertive women are never ahead of their time. Ask yourself: Are they just ahead of yours?"	You are defending against people who say assertive women are too aggressive.

Create Credibility in Tension

The last time you encountered conflict in a meeting, what happened to ease the tension? Did a leader ignore it until it dissipated? Did they tell everyone to cool down? Or did someone in the meeting turn the tension into something productive? If it was the latter, they're part of a small club of the emotionally brave.

Why, you may be wondering, is this tip to create credibility in a moment of tension in a chapter about being memorable? The answer is simple. Even if you're a woman in the junior ranks, you have power. When things get tense or heated, compliment the tension by outwardly noting how healthy contradictory viewpoints are. Solid research finds that groups of people who disagree through diversity of thought make better decisions.[21] Also, know that speaking up is more than about being memorable. It's good for your team.

What if you tried leading through conflict like this:

Colleague #1: "Why are we considering this policy change? I'm pretty concerned."

Colleague #2: "Well, I wanted to just put it out there as a possibility. We don't have to do it."

Colleague #1: "Never mind."

You: "Hold on. This is exactly the kind of discussion we need. Putting ideas out there and critiquing them is a good thing. The points you're both raising are exactly what need to be talked about."

Discomfort with disagreement is normal. When you know some will want to back off from creating more tension, make it safe for them to keep going. Your compliment defuses the awkwardness.

Create Credibility by Making Someone Who Is Frustrated Feel Heard

Like easing tension by complimenting the conflict, use your Kind Dynamite to acknowledge someone in a meeting who voices frustration. If you follow these steps to make that person feel genuinely heard, you will leave an impression on that person, *and* you will set a strong model for others around the table.

Consider the last time you were at your professional wits' end. It might not have been a game-changing project that made you so frustrated; it may have been something simple like a problem with your computer. I'll never forget how my excitement at buying my first MacBook computer turned to a desire to throw it through the window as I tried — and failed — to migrate my Outlook email from my old PC.

I called Apple tech support, already fired up with frustration, and when the completely calm technician answered the phone, my first words were something eloquent like, "Aaargh!"

She read my tone quite quickly and took me through the fixes. By the end of the conversation, I felt like we'd become friends, not only because she fixed my technical issue but because of something else I couldn't quite put my finger on.

A few hours later, I hit another roadblock, tried to solve it on my own (big mistake), and failed again. This time, I pounded the numbers on my iPhone keyboard with more verve than normal as I dialed Apple tech support again. A very enthusiastic guy answered, and once again, by the time I hung up, I felt a deep affinity for Apple (and, yes, my tech issue was resolved).

By now, I'd also realized both specialists followed a similar pattern when handling me. They did more than solve my tech problem. They made me feel seen. As a customer, that conversion from frustrated to heard made me feel loyal.

After my experience with both specialists, I believed I'd discerned the "Apple WeCare Approach" (my wording). In my head, it was a five-step approach that included a critically important first step that I rarely encountered with other tech conversations outside Apple. Just to confirm my theory, I decided I had to call Apple's tech support line a third time with a fictitious issue to test my theory. I described my fake problem, and, over the next few minutes, the third technical specialist followed my five steps beautifully.

Apple has neither confirmed nor denied the accuracy of my proud diagnosis (because I haven't yet asked them to do so), but here are the five steps for your use in a meeting, on a call, or wherever you encounter a deeply frustrated colleague or client. Again, pay particular attention to the first step because this is the one I believe so many clients skip to their detriment.

The Unsanctioned Apple WeCare Approach (As Discerned by Karen Lisko)	
Step One: Ally with the client's emotion.	"You must feel so frustrated by this point."
Step Two: Assure the client you will solve the problem together.	"We're going to figure this out."
Step Three: Solve what you can.	"The two things we can solve right now are..."
Step Four: Admit what you cannot solve in the moment and offer next steps for getting there.	"This won't fix your third hardware issue, but I'm going to send you an article to troubleshoot as well as the Genius Bar number at your nearby Apple retail store."
Step Five: Ask the client the "what else" question.[22]	"What else can I do for you before we sign off?"

That first step is the game changer. Still, in my experience, people rarely use it. I often wonder if some customer care specialists consciously avoid it. Acknowledging the customer's emotion invites more venting, and that takes time, especially when you're on a clock or know the queue is long. Allying with the customer could also scare some legal types who worry it could sound like an admission of fault for a problem. (It doesn't.)

I see many of my clients skip this important empathy step when I observe them handle frustration in meetings.

Sometimes, that avoidance is unconscious. Successful go-getters are solution-oriented. As a woman, research tells us the feminine brain (in women or in men) has the leading edge on adding empathy to that solution-oriented mindset. Many people leapfrog straight to Step Three (Solve what you can) because they see that approach as a way to satisfy the client's frustration. If *you* insist on using Step One in those interactions, you will be a memorable standout for doing so. Your superpower is to see the person, not just the problem. Try it.

Set Specific Steps

Okay, I'm just going to say it. Rather, I'm going to let Margaret Thatcher, former Prime Minister of the United Kingdom say it: "If you want something *said*, ask a man. If you want something *done*, ask a woman."

Former South Carolina governor Nikki Haley repeated this quote in 2023 when she was the only woman on the debate stage in the Republican primary race for the United States presidency. But let's sit with this quote for a minute.

We all know plenty of men who get things done. Many of my clients are men, and they accomplish a great deal day in and day out. At the same time — with no research study to back me up in the business environment — I do buy the component that women are especially good at getting things done. It's another one of our superpowers.

A recent study found that mothers do 71 percent of the mental work in the home to keep things running for the family.[23] Thinking about all the mothers I know, my first tongue-in-cheek reaction when I read the research was, "Did we really need a study to know that?"

Create Concrete Anticipation and End with Actionables

There is a special place in hell reserved for meeting agendas that focus mostly on updates and less on making decisions. Save the updates for a different forum, like an email or a memo. Updates are passive events. If you want to stand out using Kind Dynamite with your team, engage their brains in brainstorming solutions in the meeting. Create the anticipation of these steps at the *beginning* of the meeting to ensure you get a guaranteed "next."

Five Simple Steps to Productive Meetings

One never-fail approach to getting a guaranteed "next" involves five straightforward steps:

1. Launch your meeting by asking the attendees, "Where do we want to be by the end of the meeting?" Every time I start a meeting this way, the attendees never disappoint. They can get very concrete very quickly. If you've been clear in advance about the point of the meeting, they will be thinking about it before they arrive, especially if you provide advance reading material. If you want to (or, for all practical purposes, need to) assume no one will have time to read anything in advance, take a page from Amazon's book. For years, Amazon's meetings at their corporate offices have followed an approach

that starts a meeting with roughly 15 minutes of silent reading about the issue (from a thoughtfully crafted memo) to be discussed for the remaining 45 minutes. Jeff Bezos, Amazon's Founder and Chairman, credits these "silent meetings" with making discussions more productive.

2. Record the attendees' list of desired outcomes, arranging the list in real-time to follow a logical order of discussion. Remember the days of using a pad and easel for this type of task? (Okay, maybe only I remember those days.) The old-fashioned method with the smelly Sharpie marker still works, but there are added options available, especially if your meeting is via videoconference. Most platforms have a whiteboard feature that allows you to take notes for all attendees to see. Once you use it, you'll never go back.

3. Follow the list and take notes on key decisions for all to see. Make immediate judgments as attendees invariably think of other items throughout the discussion. Is the item relevant? Is there time to discuss it? If it fits better in another meeting, record it for later and honor your word to bring it up later.

4. At the end of the meeting, review the list of items with the attendees and ensure someone has been assigned to own the follow-through *with dates* for completion.

5. Share the list with all attendees after the meeting, potentially including calendar reminders of deadlines.

Convert the Client Pitch Meeting into a Strategy Session That Ends with Actionables

If you've ever pitched a client or been pitched yourself, this will sound familiar (and not in a good way). The meeting *begins* with "talking resumes," where the pitchers regale the client with their individual bios and their company's qualifications. I have seen this introductory portion last up to 15 minutes or more. No interaction with the client, no mention of the client's issues yet, just pure monologue about the great attributes of the pitch team.

Then, the pitch team gets to the issues the client is facing, but again, this part is self-focused on the team's expertise and *still* can feel like a monologue. To make matters worse, the pitch team may have a PowerPoint deck filled with bullet points that mirror the script the pitchers are using in their presentation.

How am I doing? Does this sound familiar? If your pitch team is doing more talking than the client is (which is never anyone's intent but frequently happens), you're already in bad shape. To make matters worse, even if you invited the client to ask questions at the beginning, this monologue approach says, "We don't really want you to interrupt our monologue with your questions."

Fortunately, there's an easy way to make a better, other-centered pitch to potential clients. Standing out in a client pitch starts in the early moments, even if you've met the prospective client already. *Your number one goal is to get the client talking as early (and as often) in the* conversation as possible. To make this possible, two things need to happen. First, you need to talk less, and second, you want to be ready with three key moments of questions for the client.

To talk less, skip your team's wordy introductions. You should do the bare minimum to connect the clients with the roles of each person on the pitch team and then wait to talk more about either person's expertise where it fits later in the in-depth conversation. I routinely follow this practice at speaking engagements. Even if the emcee asks me to introduce myself, I wait until a relevant point in my speech to pepper in my training and client experience. It is far better to set your bio in context later — Then it's an anecdote! — than to make it a predictable monologue at the beginning.

Three Pivotal Moments in the Pitch

To ready yourself with questions for the client, know that three pivotal moments in the pitch are perfect locations for that prepared questioning to occur.

The first moment might surprise you. That awkward small talk at the top of the meeting should not be small. The internet is a treasure trove of public information your client knows exists about themselves. The client may have volunteered the information on LinkedIn or on the company website. This means you're not "snooping" if you learn something meaningful about your client that provides a connection or a curiosity.

Did the client go to the same school as you? To a rival school where you can debate the heft of your respective sports teams? Is there a standout detail on their profile that makes you curious to know more? Before I meet with prospective clients I don't know very well, I always do this research. I then use it to connect and to subtly convey the fact that I'm detail-oriented and do my homework. Clients are typically pleased to talk about their experience rather than default to the weather, which is the universal topic of all small-talk conversations.

The second moment is an opportunity to ask a question that could drive the lion's share of your discussion in the meeting. The question I recommend you ask the prospective client is, "What's on your worry list for this matter or for this issue?"

The client is hiring you to solve a problem — or a set of them. Let the client drive these answers. Of course, you've likely thought through a few things the client *should* have on their worry list, so you can add to this list later, but let them drive first. Once you've collected their list, this gift of information is now your opportunity to turn the pitch into a strategy meeting by doing these three things:

1. Identify the services you provide that will address their worries.
2. Identify the person or team who will take the lead on each specific worry.
3. Provide some initial strategy thinking to address their worries.

Offering strategic thinking and collaboration demonstrates the critical difference between you and your competition. If you offer some advice for free, you show your generosity and your expertise (sounds like Kind Dynamite to me) in a way that few pitchers consider.

The third moment arrives when you end the pitch with a firm "ask" for the work. Your team is not casually dating this prospective client. You are looking for a firm and mutual commitment. Lead with your commitment by saying something like, "We want to work with you." Then, present your ask using an open-ended question such as:

- "What else can we tell you to handle this work for you?"
- "What else can we provide you to make your decision easy?"
- "When can we get back together to continue this conversation?"

Capitalize on your knowledge of how to stand out in a meeting and concretely how to ask for what you want. These are skills that are too rarely developed. You now have access to approaches that will work. Use them to amplify your points and your voice.

My Ask to You

I'm always working on developing what I teach profession-ally, and I could use your allyship in this effort.

I have been talking to you for many pages. Are you ready to talk to me? I'm eager to hear your honest feedback on this book, and I invite you to leave a review on Amazon. I confess that even though I teach assertiveness, I get a little tongue-tied asking for this kind of help. We are all a work in progress, it seems. My work is to trust that you will un-derstand the importance of this ask for getting the word out about this book to other women like you.

My "assertively humble" thanks,
Karen

CHAPTER 6

Step Four: Get High Credibility Marks Based on Your Delivery

When you deliver a message well, people shouldn't forget what you said, people shouldn't forget what you did, and people will never forget how you made them feel.[24]

When you think about your delivery style and the ideal Goldilocks of Kind Dynamite assertiveness, how do you know what hits the just-right balance? Importantly, what's the difference between showing up as assertive versus aggressive? Or what takes your delivery from nonassertive to assertive?

At first glance, these terms seem to be entirely subjective. Your colleagues seated around the conference table might disagree about what they define as assertive or aggressive. When I ask people, "What do you see as the difference between assertive and aggressive behavior in communication?" I get a wide variety of answers. But among those disparate answers, the most common word is *tone*.

But even tone sounds subjective! What are we supposed to do with that answer when our goal is to hit the right chord of assertiveness? Fortunately, ongoing communication research has made "what assertive communication looks and sounds like" far more concrete.

I'm about to describe the ways assertive communication can be conveyed in our delivery. We women possess the superpower to be our most effective as ourselves, rather than needing to assert ourselves like the men.

Image 2: *The Twelve Elements of Assertive Delivery*

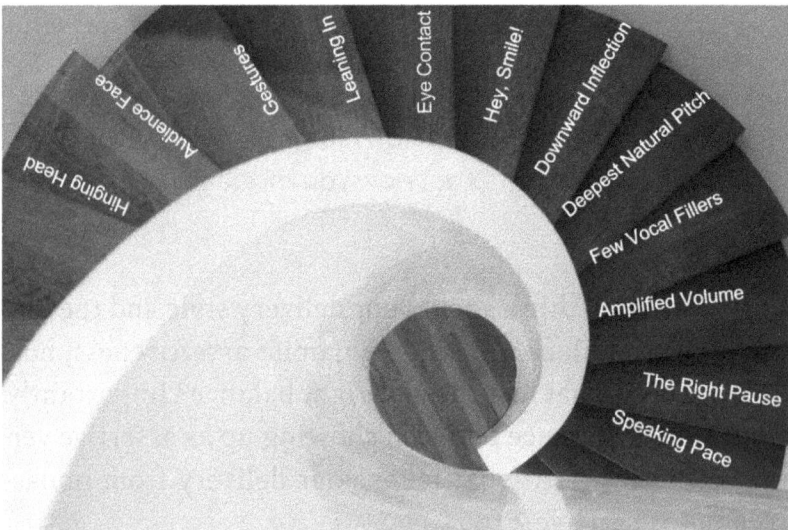

Setting aside the language you use, your tone of credible assertiveness is formulated by twelve elements of assertive delivery, including six ways you use your voice and six ways you display nonverbal behavior. All twelve elements are closely related and are what I coach high-performing professionals to recognize in themselves. They might already possess a number of these traits but don't always capitalize on them at the right moments.

You possess these elements as well. They are another key reason I named this book *Kind Dynamite*. When combined, these behaviors allow you to display your cohesive, *dynamic* manner and do so with a classy, *kind* delivery. Kindness is not weakness. It is the booster fuel of dynamism. If this sounds familiar, it should. It is a cousin of the *personable and professional* combination I described in Chapter 1.

> **Kindness is not weakness. It is the booster fuel of dynamism.**

Even though thinking about these vocal cues and nonverbal behavior one element at a time could feel strange here, keep in mind that the speaker who simply allows herself to be dynamically personable in the professional setting will authentically convey a number of the twelve elements of assertive delivery in the process.

> **The speaker who simply allows herself to be dynamically personable in the professional setting will authentically convey a number of the twelve elements of assertive delivery in the process.**

In fact, when you speak with passion about your point, you likely automatically embody a number of these elements. This chapter is all about embodying these twelve elements with intention rather than by accident.

Six Vocal Cues That Amplify Your Assertive Messaging

These six important vocal elements divide evenly into three vocal elements you should increase or amplify and three vocal elements you should decrease or lower. Think of these as the up escalators and down escalators of your tone.

DYNAMIC VOCAL "UPS"

Upend your pace
Uptick your pausing
Upsize your volume

DYNAMIC VOCAL "DOWNS"

Downsize your vocal fillers
Drop **down** your pitch
Downturn your inflection

Dynamic Vocal Element #1: Adopt a Conversational Pace

Let's start with *the* most misunderstood vocal cue by far. When people forget that their most assertive style should include a combination of personable and professional delivery, they sloooooow down their speaking pace. I've seen it happen a million times. I'll be working with an ordinarily dynamic woman, and the minute she goes into "presentation mode," she slows down her natural speaking pace. Typically, the conversation goes something like this:

Me: "Alisha, what happened to your naturally dynamic pace?"

Alisha: "I'm trying to be taken seriously."

Me: "And being dynamic makes you seem… not serious?"

Alisha: "I want to sound professional, and I'm trying to take a more sedate tone and pace. I feel like I won't be taken as seriously if I'm more upbeat."

This is the number one misconception women often have — that somehow, there exists a tradeoff between dynamism and professionalism. Not so. In fact, three decades of ongoing research have consistently found that a *slightly faster* pace of speaking is more credible in a professional setting.[25] Not rapid fire, but importantly, *not slower*. This is the first Dynamic Vocal Up: Speed up your pace!

Now, perhaps you slow down while speaking, but *unintentionally* so. We women do this for two reasons, both of which stem from a lack of belief in our message. The first reason we slow down is because of nervousness (this does speed some of us up, but I find that it *defuses* energy for most). The second reason we slow down is because we're focusing too much on precision in our messaging.

Let's look at the contrast between the two extremes of an ineffective speaking pace and an effective one. Click on the QR code below or visit karenlisko.com/videos.

Do you see how the ineffective approach may sound more serious but at the price of also sounding less energetic and even flat? The formula is quite simple. *Lower energy equals lower credibility.* More dynamite in your pace is more credible as long as you vary your rate throughout your message.

CONVERSATIONAL PACE

Poor Example:

Good Example:

Dynamic Vocal Element #2: Pause to Punctuate Your Point

If you buy what I'm selling about adopting a more dynamic pace as your default rate, this demands that you also incorporate pausing on frequent occasions. In fact, if you've ever been told to slow down, chances are good that you have *not* been speaking too fast. Rather, you may have been blurring one sentence into the next without pausing enough!

Take this as good news. It is far better to have a default rate that is moderately faster. Too many speakers overcorrect their pace by slowing down when what they need to do is to insert more silence. This is the second Dynamic Vocal Up: Turn up your vocal variety by combining a conversational pace with strategic pausing.

To be intentional with this Dynamic Vocal Up, you can use a specific method to make the good pause more impactful. When you deliver an introductory sentence, pause *and* maintain steady eye contact with your listener, going silent before you move on to the second sentence. The intentional combination of silence and eye contact communicates intent rather than nervousness. Silence is attention-getting.

Don't worry that your pause somehow miscommunicates that you've lost your place. Don't worry that someone else will hop into your spot. Your pause will not be prolonged. Trust that to you as the speaker, silence always feels longer than it does to the listener.

Take a look at the difference between an ineffective way to pause and a more effective way by clicking on the QR code below or visiting karenlisko.com/videos.

EFFECTIVE PAUSING

Poor Example:

Good Example:

In the example of effective pausing that you just watched, how do you feel the speaker's pause affected their delivery? (The speaker is me, by the way.) Did it make me look more effective?

If it looked better to you, know that it *felt* worse to me as I demonstrated effective pausing. The silence felt a little dramatic, but it helped me intentionally communicate my message.

More than one thing can be true here. You can be more effective in using silence while feeling awkward at the same time. We don't like to feel uncomfortable, and sometimes, that makes us less effective in our own delivery style. *We* may not need to pause because we know what we want to say next. But our *listeners* need us to occasionally pause because they don't.

Dynamic Vocal Element #3: Replace Your Vocal Fillers

Conversational pace? Check. Increased pausing? Check. The, um, most maddening thing many speakers battle is, like, the vocal filler. Fillers used to be narrowly defined as "uh" and "um," but present-day add-ons have expanded to include "like," "right?" and "so." Does any of this strike a chord?

What would a transcription of your speech look like? I see written transcripts a lot because a foundation of my legal work over the years has been helping witnesses find their authentic testifying voice, and witnesses' depositions and trial testimony are transcribed word for word. I have read thousands of pages of transcripts over the years, and I use them to help witnesses see their speech patterns in print. The most common vocal fillers in that setting occur in communication outside the courtroom as well — one at the beginning of sentences, one in the middle of them, and one that occurs at the end.

The preamble "so" appears at the *beginning* of far too many sentences and makes the rest of the statement sound less definitive.

- "So, yes. I thought I was in the right position to help."
- "So, what matters most is prioritizing patient care over self-protectiveness."

The interim "like" bogs down the *middle* of the sentence.

- "It was, like, what we needed to do."
- "I'm, like, pondering what to do next."

The final "right" at the *end* of far too many sentences makes declarative statements sound like questions.

- "We need to be confident about what we do next, right?"
- "There are several important elements to this issue, right?"

It likely comes as no surprise that research confirms using too many vocal fillers hurts your credibility.[26] But there is good news here, believe it or not. Research has also found that *some* vocal fillers are not that big of a deal.[27] The occasional vocal filler is more authentic in conversation and sometimes keeps a verbal placeholder for a speaker who is mid-thought. If a few "uhs" and "ums" creep in while you're speaking, don't sweat it.

If, however, too many vocal fillers enter your sentences, you'll want to do something about it. In the first Dynamic Vocal Down, you need to decrease your vocal fillers. Two major fixes will help you achieve this objective:

1. Speak at a slightly faster, conversational pace, and many of your vocal fillers will naturally disappear.
2. Get comfortable with silence as part of your messaging. Our discomfort with silence is part of why some of us use too many vocalized pauses. The point of pausing is to replace vocal fillers with the act of being quiet rather than simply telling yourself to get rid of the filler language.

Dynamic Vocal Element #4: Amplify Your Volume

When you incorporate the first three vocal elements, it would be a shame to go unnoticed simply because your volume is too low. Some of us women come equipped with softer voices, and some of us are born with vocal power! (You know who you are. Celebrate it!)

The physiology of your vocal cords contributes to your volume baseline. When you marry your conversational pace and effective pausing with a strong volume, you will own your credibility, even when your baseline voice starts out softer. This is your third Dynamic Vocal Up: Turn up that volume! There is no doubt that a stronger volume is more credible. Research found it to be true for women thirty years ago, and it is still true today.[28] [29] But *why* is it true?

Look at the contrast between these two videos by clicking on the QR code below or visiting karenlisko.com/videos.

EFFECTIVE VOLUME

Poor Example:

Good Example:

Do you see how much more convinced and, therefore, convincing I sound when I say the exact same words in the strong volume example? I believed in my words when I used a more muted voice, but my confidence didn't come across because I sounded tired and lacking in conviction.

Even though it may seem intuitive to adopt a strong volume when speaking, two key elements mute our voices. First, and ironically, we are not always the best judges of our own volume. If you've ever heard your own voice on a recording, I'll bet you don't like it. The truth is, how you sound on a recording is more accurate than how you sound inside your head.

The same is often true with volume. You may feel like you sound louder than you do to the outside world. When I coach women, I record them and then have them listen to their recordings. The lionesses' share of reactions go as follows:

Me: "Alisha, let's have you first just *listen* to your voice before you watch the video."

[I then play back the audio.]

Alisha: [Somewhat alarmed.] "Is that my voice? I hate how it sounds."

Me: "No one ever seems to like the sound of their voice. But listen to the overall conviction in your voice. Listen to your energy."

Alisha: "I sound so much quieter and flat than I thought I would."

Me: "You're not alone. Virtually everyone I coach has the same reaction when they hear themselves. *No one* likes the sound of their voice. But there is a great 'cheat' if you feel nervous or tired when you speak up in a meeting."

Alisha:	"What's that?"
Me:	*"Exaggerate* your volume. You will sound more convinced and credible if you do. Oh, and trust how you sound on the video. That *is* your voice to the outside world."

I know exaggeration works. I have seen it make a dramatic difference for so many of my female clients (and for many of my male clients as well). I also know this works because I exaggerate *my own* volume when I speak. In some larger rooms, I feel like I'm almost yelling, yet every time I ask others if it sounds that way to them, they look at me oddly and say I just sound dynamic. There you go.

Some of us overly temper our voices because we live too much in our own heads, fearing that louder means we will be seen as aggressive, shrill, strident, or shrewish. I list these words here to note that we must reject these descriptors often attributed to women (Thanks a lot, Shakespeare, a la *Taming of the Shrew.*) You won't see them return in my writing. Rather than lament being criticized as aggressive, let's own our vocal power and mainstream our strong volume so it becomes the positive norm rather than a gendered negative.

Dynamic Vocal Element #5: Reach Down for Your Deepest Natural Pitch

By now, you're louder, conversationally faster, and you're incorporating strategic pausing when you speak. Next, your voice needs to sound its most authoritative. This is the second Dynamic Vocal Down: Reach down with your pitch.

Research finds that a speaker's deeper pitch (both for females and males) is an asset.[30] That research comes from having tested different pitches when subjects watched the speaker make a short statement. More recent research that isolated the speaker to audio-only and lengthened the speaker's statement found no difference in pitch, gender, and credibility.[31]

Why would this recent research find no difference between the genders' credibility? While it is possible that the differences in the study's format could account for finding gender to not be a factor, it is also possible that this researcher's 2022 study supports what other recent research has found — a level set between men and women on credibility. The gender gap between men and women is narrowing! Deep credit goes to women who are (or have been) showing up as their most authentically assertive selves in meetings and setting the standard.

Whether these women use their deepest natural pitch by accident or by intent, it works. Look at the differences in these videos by clicking on the QR code below or visiting karenlisko.com/videos.

DEEPEST NATURAL PITCH

Poor Example:

Good Example:

I was one of those "high pitchers" in my youth. Then, I reviewed my own research findings and those of other social scientists concluding that a lower pitch is more credible, and I started working to find my lowest natural pitch.

We do not have to talk like the men to achieve this! Take a second look at the deeper pitch video. You will see that I was holding my hand to my sternum when I spoke. That action allowed me to feel the vibration of my lowest natural pitch and ensure I was at that physiological point. I urge you to try the same technique. If you feel vibration coming through your fingers as you speak, congratulations. You have found *your* deepest natural pitch!

Dynamic Vocal Element #6: End with Downward Inflection

The third Dynamic Vocal Down is one of the most important switches we women need to make. Often called "upspeak," upward inflection is that tendency to sound like you're asking a question when you aren't as you end a declarative sentence. You know it when you hear it, and then *you can't stop hearing it.* Too often, we notice it in others but not in ourselves.

The next time you tell someone your cell number or email address, listen to your inflection. "My email address is karen@karenlisko.com?" It sounds like I'm questioning my own email address.

Take a listen to the upward inflection video and then immediately compare it to the downward inflection video by clicking on the QR code below or visiting karenlisko.com/videos.

DOWNWARD INFLECTION

Poor Example:

Good Example:

The consequences of us using an upward inflection range from a minor credibility hit to a more serious perception issue. The credibility hit comes from the upward inflection, converting your language from powerful to powerless. The more serious issue is that it calls forward "linguistic misogyny," which inaccurately frames women who speak with this speech pattern as "stupid."[32]

Here's some good news laced with only a modicum of bad news. The good news is that you can readily self-diagnose whether you have a habit of using upward inflection. The bad news is that there is only one way to reach that diagnosis. You need to become annoyed with your upward inflection, which requires audio recording yourself and catching yourself in the act. I *don't* expect you will like it. At the same time, I *do* expect you'll love yourself for correcting it.

Pull It All Together and Vary It!

There was a method to my madness in talking about each vocal element separately. It's the best way I know to teach the powerful way we women can use our voices. But that isn't the end of it. Of course, when you talk, you use volume, pitch, rate, and the rest all at the same time. So, how do these disparate elements intersect most effectively? There's one answer: Through variety! For example:

- Vary your pace and insert pausing for effect.
- Occasionally lower your volume for emphasis.
- Vary your deeper pitch. Research finds that varying your pitch grabs and keeps a listener's attention. Being emphatic increases your credibility.[33] Picture yourself using a matter-of-fact tone in an energetic manner. That is the best way I know how to note that you want to use your lowest natural pitch while being dynamic. *That* hits the holy grail of pitch and persuasiveness.

If you're a visual person and want a separate way to think about vocal variety, try this trick: Verbally **boldface**, underline, and *italicize* certain words in your message, just as you might in writing. (And, no, I'm not being literal and suggesting that you write out your comments.) Verbally "punch" certain words by bolding a phrase with your volume or by underlining a word with a different pitch.

You do these things naturally when you feel passionate about your subject. Use this technique when you're in a meeting, and you'll stand out for your conviction, even if you feel a bit over the top in your delivery. Remember, it may feel uncomfortable to you, but it won't come across as too dramatic to your listeners.

Six Effective Nonverbals You Can Use from Your Seat

Let's move to the way you appear when you deliver smart messaging. Nonverbal communication can either amplify or distract from your words. It matters deeply and is usually the first impression we make.

Our nonverbal impressions can also differ by gender, but again, we must be very careful to stay current on how those differences appear. In our rapidly changing gender dynamics in professional settings, older research from the twentieth century can be unreliable. Women show up differently in meetings today and are perceived differently as well. And when it comes to reading nonverbal communication in others, I have current news! We women read others' nonverbals more accurately than men do![34]

It's funny how we typically think of our nonverbal communication *a lot* when presenting on our feet but rarely when sitting in a meeting or on a videoconference. Nonverbal communication from your seat is still deeply important when you care about credibility and persuasiveness (and when don't you?). Four of the nonverbal cues I'm going to teach you count when you're speaking, and two matter most when you're listening.

The Speaker's Nonverbal Element #1: Smile!

I was in Chicago recently to work with an expert witness on her courtroom testimony for an upcoming jury trial. Her content wasn't funny. (That wasn't the goal.) It wasn't lighthearted, and it wasn't exciting. (That is a reality with most expert testimony.) She was testifying about monetary damages in a patent case. And, still, our conversation went something like this:

Me:	"Jayne, you're so 'user friendly' with the jury when describing your damages model, but you look unapproachable when you talk about it."
Jayne:	"Well, thanks, I guess, for the user-friendly compliment. But what do you mean by unapproachable, and why does that even matter in this context? I'm here to educate the jury about the problem with the other side's numbers."
Me:	"Exactly! Your job is to make the jury feel smarter, not dumber. Jurors often feel intimidated by the numbers in a civil case, and the last thing you want them to take away from your demeanor is that this is weighty stuff that requires the same PhD you possess to understand it. They will feel less intimidated if you focus on putting them at ease. Smiling at appropriate points will make them warm up to you and feel more relaxed about your testimony."

Jayne: "I suppose that makes sense. I still remember one of my favorite finance professors in school who made the content interesting by putting more personality into his teaching. Is that what you mean?"

Me: "That is *exactly* what I mean! In a courtroom or a boardroom, it is especially important to stand out by being personable *and* professional. Your audience will learn better, and you will be seen as a confident authority on the matter."

You don't have to smile your way through your entire message. That would be odd. Bordering on creepy, even. But if you think of your role as "hosting your comment," your natural warmth will appear. Know that smiling is *a direct sign* of credibility.[35] By contrast, a straight-faced, all-business demeanor can be misinterpreted as nervousness.

The Speaker's Nonverbal Element #2: Make Kind Dynamite Eye Contact

When you smile, does it reach your eyes? In what we all might categorize in the "obviousness" column, making effective eye contact reads as confident.[36] But a deeper layer exists when thinking about eye contact, credibility, and women. Some research has found that men more frequently use domineering eye contact (a prolonged gaze with furrowed brow) with lower-powered individuals.[37] Historically (but decreasingly so), women have had less power than men. But even when women have greater power, we tend to use domineering eye contact less than men. That's a great thing since its intent is to diminish the other person.

Does domineering eye contact qualify as Kind Dynamite? Nope. Is there a better way? Yes. Return to the "dinner host" analogy I've been using throughout this book. When you know your role in a meeting is to put your listeners at ease, your eye contact necessarily becomes both steady and kind, even when matters can get heated.

The Speaker's Nonverbal Element #3: Literally Lean In

Strong eye contact and an animated face deserve to be coupled with an assertive posture. In a fitting homage to Sheryl Sandberg, who authored the iconic book *Lean In*, the *nonverbal* corollary of how you lean into a meeting conversation adds to Sandberg's advice to philosophically lean into your professional power as a woman. Leaning in physically requires a triad of steps to effectively use your upper body:

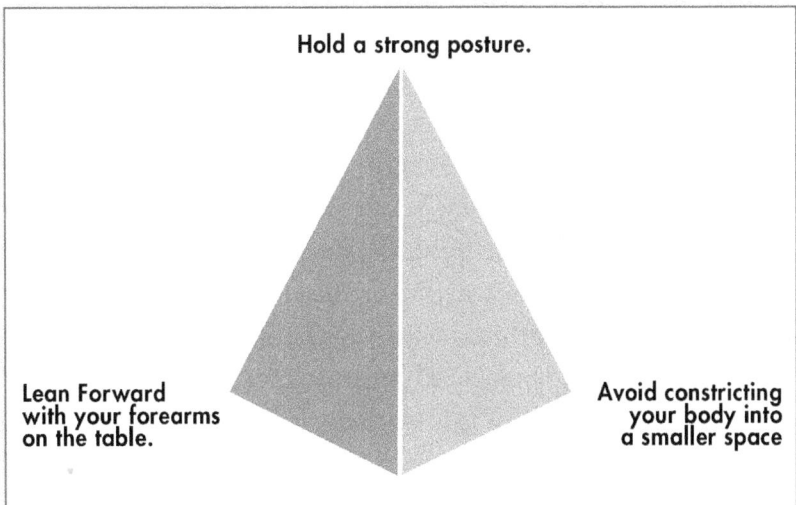

Hold a strong posture.

Lean Forward with your forearms on the table.

Avoid constricting your body into a smaller space

To begin using your body effectively during meetings, I want you to do a simple test. The next time you sit down at a conference table, take a "torso inventory." Where is your body leaning? Are you hunched over? Are you doing something called asymmetrical positioning (which means you're leaning to one side or another)? *Does it even matter?* It does. Research that focuses specifically on the meeting setting finds that nonverbal behavior enhances or diminishes the trustworthiness of a speaker's message. The impact on employee engagement is real. Researchers found that "[T]he better the employee can understand and trust the leader, the higher the likelihood that the team member speaks [their] mind more freely.[38]

You have worked too hard to make your words trustworthy to reduce that trust with poor body language. Trustworthiness is directly linked to a number of nonverbals, including your use of your torso. If you lean into the conversation with good posture, forearms on the table, and open hands, your body conveys engagement. Of course, the way you use your voice can either enhance or diminish your nonverbals too. It's all a package deal!

If you've ever had the misfortune of being assigned the middle seat on a full airline flight, you've likely had to maneuver the "armrest power play." There is no dedicated set of armrests for the middle seater, so the dance is to determine who gets the rights to which armrest. Research (and personal experience) tells us that men tend to expand into armrest space *and* other meeting spaces. That same research finds that we women tend to contract into our spaces.[39] Unfortunately, this also applies to conference rooms, stages, and anywhere else you find yourself addressing an audience.

My fervent hope is that just knowing this research will empower you to expand! If you need more motivation, know that taking up more space communicates confidence and power. Shrinking into your space communicates the opposite. In 2012, social psychologist Amy Cuddy's TED Talk went viral when she introduced the "power pose," which translates as standing or sitting in an expansive posture of confidence.[40] In fact, her TED Talk video has been viewed more than 73 million times. Some social scientists dispute parts of her claims, but 73 million views tell you people are more than a little intrigued about the topic.

The Speaker's Nonverbal Element #4: Use Hand Gestures Well

When you lean forward, try to continue using your hands to gesture as you speak. Talking with our hands is something some of us do well and something some of us hate. I'm asked repeatedly, "What do I do with my hands when I'm speaking?"

To which I respond, "What do you *usually* do with your hands?"

My question is usually met with a look of bewilderment.

This short interaction played out over and over proves that we at once care about what we do with our hands while being woefully unaware of what our baseline "hand talking" even looks like.

Recent research has found that talking with your hands a moderate amount enhances your appearance of confidence and credibility.[41] You get extra points for incorporating some illustrative gestures as you speak. This gesture concretely supplements the language you use, such as holding up three fingers when you say you have three points. Don't overdo it. You don't need to pantomime your entire message! But don't underdo it either by locking your hands in a death grip. Let your gestures happen, and don't overthink it.

The Listener's Nonverbal Element #1: The Active-Audience Face

Okay, look. Literally. Most of those who teach nonverbals focus only on what your body is up to when you're *speaking*. But remember, we still create nonverbal impressions when we *listen*. And there's a problem. When most of us are listening to someone else speak in a meeting, we typically default into "audience mode," especially when more than two of us are in the meeting. We aren't looking at ourselves (unless we are sitting in gallery view in a videoconference), and we too easily forget that others just might be looking at us as we sit in audience mode.

I blame public speaking courses (which I taught for years at the college level and still teach in the private sector). I say this rather tongue-in-cheek because it isn't *really* our fault. But think about it. In public speaking courses, we focus on our "speaking faces," but no one teaches us anything about "public audiencing."

In my line of work, I'm in a lot of meetings. I spend some of my time watching non-speakers in the meeting. I'm not alone. Your colleagues are watching you and one another. And remember, your female colleagues may be especially attuned to listeners around the table,` given the research that we women are more astute readers of nonverbal communication.[42]

From what I can tell, most listeners seem to think they're invisible when their mouths aren't moving. Guess what? *We can still see you.* When you're checking your phone during an in-person meeting, *we see you.* In virtual meetings, *we can see you* reading your email on a side monitor! Alternatively, listeners might be off their side electronic devices, but their faces are blank or disengaged. And thin-slice research tells us that we are still conveying credibility impressions of ourselves as we sit silently in the meeting.[43]

To this end, the first nonverbal element you need to master as a listener is developing your "listening face." We women tend to have more expressive faces (another superpower of ours), so if you fall into the category of already being more expressive, you're ahead of the game.[44] You will help your own credibility by showing engaged interest in the person speaking and by conveying nonverbal reactions to what the speaker is saying.

The added benefit to enhancing your own credibility is that the speaker will likely appreciate you for your visual engagement. Many speakers gauge their own effectiveness by the responsiveness of those they're addressing. Unfortunately, we often overthink people's nonverbal unresponsiveness (remember, no one took a course in "public audiencing"), and many of us feel we did poorly because listeners don't show much reaction when they're listening. Listeners typically don't think they have a responsibility to show visual engagement. But now that you've read this book, you know something most people don't. Use it to your advantage.

The Listener's Nonverbal Element #2: The Hinging Head

No, that isn't a typo. I did *not* mean "hanging head." I fully meant "hinging head," as in a hinge that moves.

You may think, *Ah. You mean nodding. Isn't that over-done?* Nodding researchers (yes, that's right, it's a special-ty) find that nodding at an appropriate level builds trust and liking.[45] Most people warm to the person who nods in a meeting, seeing it as an encouraging sign that someone is listening *and* is with them. (It turns out that is not always the case, but it can feel that way.) So, yes, nodding is a great way to "hinge" your head up and down.

There is a second important way to hinge. Take a page from the book of the co-anchors of your favorite televised news or sports broadcast. These co-anchors have been trained to look to their side toward their cohost to show nonverbal engagement rather than simply looking straight ahead at the camera. This matters. I have coached several "pitch teams" over the years (those who are in the finals to pitch a prospective client for work) and I continue to see teams make the initial mistake of looking straight ahead at the client without appearing to take in what the col-league to the left or right is saying. When you acknowledge your speaking colleague, you nonverbally convey a sense of team. Clients notice these small signs.

Trust Your Kind Dynamite Instincts

Here's the good news: You likely already use a number of these twelve elements of assertive delivery to create credibility when you care deeply about your topic and are respectfully engaged in thoughtful conversation with someone. *That* is Kind Dynamite. Don't isolate these behaviors to personal conversations. Instead, use these behaviors in the meeting setting.

When your meeting is by videoconference, trust that you may need to emphasize these behaviors even more since the transmission of your presence to your viewer's screen loses some dynamism in the process (more on this in Chapter 10). Your effort will pay off, even when you initially feel you're "wearing" some of these behaviors like an "extroversion coat." You *will* warm into these behaviors in a way that feels genuine and looks credible.

CHAPTER 7

Step Five: Persuade Those Polarized Against You

Democracy falters not when we disagree about things but when we lose interest in trying to make sense of the other person's point of view and in trying to persuade that person of the merit of our own.

— Kwame Anthony Appiah

Disagreement at work is inevitable when smart, independent people come together. Research finds that it can also be deeply frustrating.[46] Think of how much easier your day would be if everyone thought and talked exactly like you! Then, think about how boring that life would be.

Disagreement is not something to dread. Handled well, it is something to race toward. As I just described in the previous chapter, there are so many ways disagreement can be productive when people are willing to voice different solutions to the same work problem. And the downsides of having no disagreement or avoiding it significantly outweigh the temporary peace you may enjoy.

Increasingly, though, we seem to encounter not just a difference in opinion but outright polarization at home, at work, and on the world stage. The first time I noticed the word *polarization* being thrown about more than just occasionally in the national media was during the 2016 presidential election between Democratic candidate Joe Biden and Republican candidate Donald Trump. It turns out the word *polarization* has been around for far longer. (Think about the Civil Rights Act of 1964 and the Vietnam Conflict, to name just two historically polarizing events.) Still, the word seemed to become a frequent household term during the 2016 election. Not surprisingly, many blame politicians for the term's common usage.

I wanted to dig deeper into the history of the word *polarization* to fine-tune my advice on persuading those whose views might be the opposite of yours. My archeological research finds two types of polarization (as if we need even one). The first is called ideological polarization. This is the type connected to policy and politics. The second is called affective polarization, meaning an emotional dislike for someone's identity. This dislike is often attributed to a dislike for a political party, but it can also bleed into a dislike for a religion, sexual identity, or nationality. An in-depth article about polarization, misperceptions, and research findings written by Rachel Kleinfeld in 2023 is worth a deep read.[47]

Think about these words: Party. Religion. Identity. Race. Nationality. These are all nouns. As a researcher who focuses on the power of language, I'm most concerned with the fact that the worst of our narrowing happens when we see a person *only* as a noun. When we think we know all we need to know about someone as a group noun (the label), we stop working to understand them as an individual noun (the person). It is tragic. It stalls dialogue. It stymies growth. Affective polarization also thrives on misperceptions by both sides. Add the fact that affective polarization is emotional, and we risk avoidance of one another on one end of the spectrum or explosiveness toward one another on the other.

In 2017, Professor Lynn Vavrek summarized long-running research that found a dramatic increase over a nearly six-decade span (between 1958 and 2016) in parents' wishes that their daughter marry someone of the same political party.[48] While political party is simply one marker of polarization, this finding is telling. In an era where tolerance of diverse backgrounds and viewpoints is arguably on the rise in many places, this decrease in the surveyed parents' tolerance for political parties to cross-marry appears in sharp contrast. Vavrek refers to this as "political tribalism."[49]

Is there a better way to face polarizing issues in the workplace, especially when your goal is to be persuasive about a work issue or decision? Is there something you can do using the feminine brain and compassionate directness (otherwise known as Kind Dynamite)? There is. To take on all dimensions of polarization in the workplace would take an entire book. Fortunately, those books have been written. I recommend to you the profound wisdom of three authors I deeply respect on this issue: Dolly Chugh, author of *The Person You Mean to Be,* and coauthors Kenji Yoshino and Dan Glasgow, who wrote *Say the Right Thing: How to Talk About Identity, Diversity, and Justice.*[50]

In this chapter, I will arm you with ways to better understand the perspectives of those you feel are outside your persuasive reach and strategies to authentically appeal to them using Kind Dynamite. To do so, I'll be borrowing some wisdom from the authors I just recommended to you.

Understand Your Tougher Audience's Mindset

One effortless way to walk through life is to surround yourself with people who think and act exactly as you do. Agreement doesn't usually keep us up at night the way conflict does. It also might just be a pretty hollow way to live if you care about growing your perspective. At a minimum, think about how boring it would be! Yet, many of us gravitate to this kind of community — less conflict, less pushing against your perspectives, more validation of how you see the world.

I vividly remember presenting to a group of attorneys a few years ago on the topic of persuading the polarized. As I stood at the head of a very long conference table in an all-glass conference room at the top of a spectacular, high-rise building, one smart attorney raised his hand and said, "Why on earth would I want to engage in conversation with someone whose political beliefs are different than mine?"

I remember seeing my reflection in one of the glass windows at that moment, and my face clearly showed my shock at his question (speechlessness, much to my children's chagrin, is not a common occurrence for me). I wish I could tell you I converted him with my response, but I never saw him again, so I don't know if he stayed his course or if he branched out. Still, I did my best to appeal to him as my tougher audience in that moment.

Look, I get it. It can make your head hurt to have to defend your position on a controversial issue. Sometimes, you just want a martini and an easy conversation (or maybe just the martini). What challenges you about your own belief system if not others' questions? When you look back at the growth points in your life, did they happen when topics were safe and easy? Or did they happen when discussions were scratchy? Standing still in life or pushing forward. Which do you choose?

In full disclosure, I'm in a politically mixed marriage. Let me tell you, it can be trying, especially during election years. I sometimes envy those couples who seem so aligned about their political views, and I suspect my husband of 35 years feels the same! Trust me, I'm not one to hand out relationship advice, but when people ask me how we make it work, my answer is simple: deep respect, a lot of listening, a little tongue-biting, and the willingness to get mad at one another. We don't have to agree on everything (what couple does?), but we do work hard at listening rather than feeling betrayed that our better half doesn't share our political bent. The easy thing would be to avoid the conversations altogether. But I've learned the hard way that avoiding conflict often grows conflict over time.

Rachel Kleinfeld summarized another truth beautifully in her article about polarization. Significant research finds that we have more in common than we know with those we believe are our opposite. We can see our differences in such bright lights that we get blinded to our commonalities.

Still, differences in ideology do exist, and if we want to persuade those who have different viewpoints, we'll need to do more than make our favorite arguments that would persuade those who are already like us. We probably get plenty of practice honing those arguments in our side conversations! When you need to persuade a room — virtual or in person — you need to focus on those who are either neutral or initially opposed to you. Those who are with you don't need your persuasive efforts. They're already on your side!

So, how do you get into the minds of your tougher audience? Two ways:

1. *Diagnose* them when you truly know them well.
2. *Research* them when you don't!

Diagnose Your Tougher Audience When You Know Them Well

Reality check. You may believe you know someone well who is part of your tougher audience, but do you truly, honestly know the person or persons you need to persuade? Is there any chance you have either an outdated or biased view of the person? Here are five completely non-research-based ways to check in with yourself:

1. Do you catch yourself frequently thinking about the person as a common noun (the person's group) rather than as a proper noun (the individual)?

2. Are you deeply frustrated by the person's strong position on one key topic?
3. Does the person remind you strongly of someone you don't like?
4. Do you still feel stung by a prior conversation with this person?
5. Has it been a while since you had an in-depth conversation with this person on an ideological issue (or if you never have, are you relying on a third person's description of the person)?

If your answer to any of these questions is "yes," I'll be blunt: Your knowledge of the person is probably clouded, and you need to dig deeper.

If, on the other hand, you still feel you see the person clearly, then move to diagnosis. I'm a fan of using something Kenji Yoshino and David Glasgow created called The Controversy Scale.[51]

The Controversy Scale				
Tastes	**Facts**	**Policies**	**Values**	**Equal Humanity**
Food Music	Data Historical Events	Rules Laws	Ethics Religion	Views of LGBTQ+ Individuals

Least Controversial   Most Controversial

Here's how this works:

1. Think of a controversial work issue where you want to persuade the tougher audience.
2. Identify where *you* land on the scale.
3. Identify where you think the tougher-audience *individual* lands on the scale.

Let's try this with a business example. First, the controversial work issue. Let's say you work in the health-care field, and you want to put budget dollars toward an LGBTQ-specific outreach program to address this group's specific healthcare concerns. Your tougher-audience person resists, saying company policy is that no affinity groups should get additional budget dollars beyond what was already budgeted for the year. You are frustrated at being turned down and want to try to change the policy in a meeting with the individual and others.

Now, your job is to identify where you see yourself on the controversy scale. Perhaps you see this issue falling squarely in the Equal Humanity category. You want the LGBTQ affinity group to be afforded this money for an arguably important reason, especially as a way to endorse these individuals' value within the company.

Finally, identify where you see the tougher-audience individual on the controversy scale. You may feel their "no more dollars for this affinity group" response is discriminatory. But the individual likely sees themself in the Policy segment. Knowing where you both land on the scale gives you information you can use to make a Kind Dynamite argument to persuade your tougher audience (more on this later in the chapter).

Research Your Tougher Audience When You Don't Know Them Well

Before we move to how to authentically appeal to your tougher audience, let's address the more likely scenario where you either don't know your tougher audience at all or you know them only slightly. The only way to combat seeing them as a common noun (i.e., their labels) is to get to know them as their proper noun (i.e., as their individual selves). There are two scenarios to consider when doing this, and it comes down to whether you get advance access to them before the meeting.

To give you an example of what I mean, I'm going to depart the conference room setting for a moment and visit the courtroom. A recent trial team asked me to advise them during jury selection about who to question and who to strike from the jury panel. I'd designed attitudinal questions for jurors that went beyond mere demographics and had also watched the potential jurors closely when the attorneys questioned them. As I prepared to advise the trial team about who to strike, local counsel suddenly appeared at trial counsel's side and whispered, "You should strike Juror Seven. He lives in a rural county and won't have opinions about the contract issues in a way that favors us."

Translation? Local counsel was looking at Juror Seven as a common noun — a rural juror who was too naïve to understand our side's contract arguments. Local counsel didn't know this Juror Seven; he was simply making judgments by thinking of the juror as his geography.

At this point, I intervened, disagreeing with local counsel's generic assumptions, and argued to keep Juror Seven since we knew his specific reactions during jury selection. His geography absolutely did not limit his intellect. We know from decades of research that people are more than their demographics, more than their gender, and more than their education level. Yet, too often, we begin and end our assessments of people based on their categories or common nouns. (By the way, we kept Juror Seven.)

You do not want to make this mistake with a tougher-audience colleague or client. The more you learn about the person's attitudes, the better equipped you will be to make arguments that appeal to the person's judgments. If you have advance access to the person, consider asking them about their initial thoughts before the meeting. Don't engage in an argument; simply view your role as a curious questioner and listen to their response. If you don't have advance access to the person, talk with others who know the individual well. However, you must be careful, as others could see the person through a biased lens.

Set Realistic Goals About Persuading Your Tougher Audience

Think way back to Chapter 1. Remember the barrier some people unfortunately put up by thinking, *My argument won't change the person anyway, so why bother speaking up?* And if you recall my counter-argument (or even if you don't), I countered that your argument may still be worth verbalizing because it could change someone near that person *and*, at a minimum, it could change *you*. It is much too easy to stay silent in a controversial moment and much too difficult to regret holding your tongue.

You may not fundamentally change your tougher audience, at least not in the moment. But you'll still succeed in planting the seeds of a new idea or perspective. If you've ever encountered someone whose initial reaction is to resist your idea only to percolate on it to the point of resisting it less (or even agreeing to it) down the road, you know it can be literally groundbreaking to raise an argument, even if building the blocks of your idea must come later.

Social psychologist Dr. Dolly Chugh does a brilliant job summarizing a model of persuasion called the 20/60/20 rule in her book, *The Person You Mean to Be: How Good People Fight Bias*.[52] Dr. Chugh credits Global Change Consultant Susan Lucia Annunzio for introducing her to the concept. She describes three different types of people in organizations when it comes to effecting change. There are the 20 percent who are with you. There are the 20 percent who will actively resist you. And there are the 60 percent she calls the "movable middle."

Sometimes, the 60 percent are the quiet ones. Do not mistake their quietude for a lack of interest. They may seem passive, and some may claim to be. They may be watchful, wanting more information or fearing controversy. My best advice? Assume they are listening and assume they need you. This latter point is not arrogance. It is empowerment. They may not all end up agreeing with you, but believing you have a right to speak up will embolden your confidence.

Make Kind Dynamite Arguments Aimed Toward Your Tougher Audience

Alright, enough about understanding your tougher audience's mindset. Let's get to work framing your argument. The genius of the 20/60/20 rule is that it acknowledges it is the rare team that is one hundred percent in lock step. Even a group of people attending the same political rally is diverse. It would be a superficial mistake to assume their attendance means they see every issue similarly to the person standing to the left or right of them.

This reality means you would be wise to consider the portions of the team that need your persuasive efforts most. Logic would dictate that the 20 percent who are with you need your efforts the least. Yet, the biggest mistake I see clients initially make is framing their arguments mainly for their allies. In fact, they may have even run their arguments past some of those allies to get their feedback. That is a *big* mistake. The 60 percent in the moveable middle and some in the polarized 20 percent need your persuasive efforts far more.

The cool thing about this step is that we can merge Yoshino and Glasgow's Controversy Scale with Chugh's 20/60/20 summary to figure out a better approach. Let's pick the earlier example back up where your goal is to persuade a colleague that the LGBTQ affinity group in your company should get extra budgetary dollars for a healthcare initiative. You see this issue as one of acknowledging the equal humanity of the group, while the polarized tougher audience describes their objection as one of policy.

The Backfire Approach

First, let's look at a "backfire approach" that insists your tougher audience see things through *your* equal humanity position on the scale. In this scenario, you respond to your colleague by saying, "I can't believe you're hiding behind policy when you're clearly discriminating against the LGBTQ affinity group. What kind of person are you?"

In this statement, you've made an automatic assumption that the person's objection is about devaluing the humanity of the affinity group. Is it possible that person is acting from a point of discrimination? Yes, it's possible. But you might also be dead wrong. Consider the probability that you do not know that person's story.

The Basic Kind Dynamite Approach

Now, let's try an approach that meets your tougher audience at *their* policy position on the scale. In this scenario, you respond by saying, "You say the policy of disallowing extra budget dollars for the LGBTQ affinity group is based on budget policy. You may not know that the LGBTQ affinity group's plan is to throw a fundraiser to raise awareness. That means the company budget will benefit because the expenses incurred for that fundraiser can be deducted. Given that new information, might I suggest that you update the policy to allow the LGBTQ affinity group to carry on?"

Why does this qualify as a Kind Dynamite approach? It is *kind* because you educated the resistant party about the fundraiser plan without being condescending. It is *dynamite* because you confidently asserted your "ask" of updating the policy to extend to the LGBTQ affinity group *and* to all other groups that incorporate a fundraising approach.

The Advanced Kind Dynamite Approach

To reach the next level, let's supplement your message by adding a Curiosity Filter from Chapter 2 and incorporating the impromptu Triple W structure from Chapter 4.

Curiosity Filter	"What if I told you I know a way to update the policy to save the company money through *more* budget expenditures?"
What is the issue?	"The LGBTQ affinity group wants to have a fundraiser to raise awareness."
Why is it significant?	"Making this a fundraiser enables the company to write off expenses as a necessary and reasonable business expense."
Where does that leave the company?	"If you update this policy, it will allow more than just the LGBTQ affinity group to throw fundraisers. Other affinity groups could do the same."
Return to the Curiosity Filter	"So, the courage to update the policy honors the affinity groups and enhances our company's reputation through our fundraising efforts. You would get that credit."

Use Your Compassionate Directness in Conflict

By now, it is my fervent hope that you see opposition and conflict as opportunities rather than as something to avoid. When you approach the situation with compassionate directness (a.k.a. Kind Dynamite), you will feel more in control, you will be seen more credibly, and you might just get your way. As women, we have an extra superpower to combine these elements and bring them to controversy.

Step Six: Influencing Up When Managing Difficult Circumstances and Difficult Personalities

The best formula for remaining a victim is to keep complaining about difficult people and take no action. You must do something different if you want to take control.

We're friends by now, right? (We've made it to Chapter 8, after all.) I have a secret to confess. For all my communication chops, I've been at my worst when communicating up, especially when the "up" (my boss or client) was intimidating or difficult. But I believe the people with whom we struggle the most are the ones who teach us the most about ourselves.

I'll never forget the first time I realized I had a "backing down" problem to solve — and quickly. I was a 27-year-old trial consultant in yet another conference room, this time in Portland, Oregon, advising an attorney on his preparation of a criminal defendant who was standing trial for rape. Despite being new to consulting on cases like this, I knew two things exceptionally well. First, I knew a lot about effective witness communication since it was a prominent part of my doctoral training. Second, I knew (as do all attorneys) that the golden rule of witness preparation is to compel the witness to always tell the truth.

I met the witness, who came across as mild-mannered, and his criminal defense attorney, who was gruff and no-nonsense. As a young woman, I already felt intimidated, but I knew it was my job to compartmentalize my fear. About an hour into the preparation session, we decided to do some mock questioning so the witness could understand how the style of courtroom questions differs from conversational ones.

The witness answered a series of questions, and things started to feel off. I brushed my first impression aside, and we continued. Several minutes later, my gut again communicated with my brain that something was wrong. I called for a break and took the attorney out into the hallway.

Here's how that conversation went:

Me:	"It feels to me that your client is lying."
Criminal Defense Attorney:	"Well, if you're accusing me of advising him to lie, I haven't."
Me:	"Oh! I'm sure you haven't. I'm just saying his testimony is off. He isn't being consistent."
Criminal Defense Attorney:	"He might not be consistent, but that doesn't mean he's a rapist. You know, some of the nicest people I know are accused of sexual assault."
Me:	[Taken aback by his "nicest people" comment.] "Okay, well..."
Criminal Defense Attorney:	"Look, we're paying you by the hour. You're not cheap, and my client doesn't have a lot of money! Can we just get back in there?"

This was my moment of truth. Was I misreading the witness? If I was right about my gut reaction, should I go back in there and help his client prepare to lie? Mind you, I'd been a stellar follower of directions given by parents and (mostly male) professors for 27 years. This attorney — my client — was in a position of authority at that moment, and I was well-versed in people pleasing. Was the client always right, as the adage suggests?

I looked at the attorney, took a deep breath, and in a quivering voice, said, "I'm stopping this session. I'm not going to help your witness lie."

In that instant, I was equal parts terrified and proud. I might have blacked out after that because, though I know the session ended, I frankly don't recall what the attorney said to me next. I know he wasn't pleased. I do recall, however, that my boss had my back when I relayed the story to her later.

I'm relieved to tell you two things have happened since. First, to my knowledge, I have not experienced another situation where the attorney and witness showed up prepared to lie or left with that same intent. Despite their stereotypically questionable reputation, most attorneys take their ethics oaths seriously. I constantly hear them tell their witnesses they must tell the truth. Second, I knew I had to figure out a way to handle other intimidating clients who would surely cross my path.

I started researching approaches to dealing with circumstances I would find difficult and difficult personalities who would challenge my professional circumstances. I learned a lot, tested what I learned with more success than failure, and now teach these principles. This chapter will summarize those lessons.

Mastering Challenging Circumstances when Managing Up

The very phrase "managing up" means you manage a challenging role — your own. When I advise clients on how to "advise up," they typically tell me they struggle with three common scenarios:

1. **How to brief business leaders** who don't know 90 percent of what I know and who only give me 10 percent of their time to understand how my subject matter affects their bottom line.

2. **How to say "no"** to un-doable requests without fearing my role is at risk.
3. **How to handle pushback** from a strong personality who is in a position superior.

Challenge #1: Briefing and Persuading Business Leaders

Persuading others in meetings can feel much different when the object of your persuasive efforts is your boss. Even if you have a terrific rapport with your boss (lucky you), the subject matter could be challenging. Or you may need to communicate with your boss's boss(es). And just to keep things interesting, perhaps you must brief this group on something they think very little about on a daily basis but care very much about if it affects the bottom line. Sound familiar? This kind of communication requires a specific finesse.

Your role is to teach your boss (or your boss' boss) in a way that gets your message across in a useful way. Often, your biggest challenge is your wealth of knowledge. A busy business leader cannot listen to your entire download as much as you might love what you know. Guess what's coming? Remember the Triple W argument structure from Chapter 4? It's exactly what you need here.

Let's prove it through two scenarios.

Sample Scenario #1: You Want to Persuade Executive Leadership to Invest in a Counterintuitive Solution

One of the best uses of the What/Why/Where model is when you want to advocate a counterintuitive solution.

What is the counterintuitive solution?	"Our brand is losing steam, so we need to behave in a growth manner."
Why is that important?	"By showing the public we are expanding, we will increase confidence in the strength of our brand."
Where does that leave the company?	"The company's initial investment in loss should result in ten-fold growth."

In this example, the *What* spotlights a contrast between loss and gain. Your current scenario may not be about loss and gain, but you will get focused attention if you use contrast as a device to make your point. Our brains love contrast. All of those "before and after" real estate shows can't be wrong. The contrast of good and evil is the bedrock of Hollywood movies. The beauty of contrast is that you can convey it in a word-efficient single sentence.

Sample Scenario #2: You Need to Deliver Bad News to Executive Leadership

The value of a tightly built message, when you need to deliver bad news, is that it gives executive leadership a complete picture in a time-efficient way. The bigger mistake occurs when you believe you need to give a more detailed background to management, which leads too slowly to your punch line. In the American culture, bottom-lining your point up front (the *What*) is the more likely way to get and keep management's attention. It also sounds more courageous.

What is the issue?	"Our department fell short of its goals, and it happened at the perfect time."
Why is it significant?	"That shortfall made us dig deeper, and we learned our department has had redundant responsibilities with another department at one of our other locations."
Where does that leave the company?	"The company will make more money if we put the two departments under one umbrella."

In this scenario, articulating the *Why* and the *Where* reveals you to be a proactive team member who has already begun the process of troubleshooting next steps. It is far better to be concise even when there is much more you could add. When you know your executive team is comprised of some who want a lot of detail and some who only want the bare facts, it is still advisable to be efficient with your words. You can always offer more detail, and management can always ask for more detail if they wish.

Challenge #2: Delivering a Helpful "No" in a Meeting

"If I never say 'no,' my yeses become less meaningful."

These are wise words that I've had to take to heart as a recovering "yes woman." Can you relate? The predictable pattern of agreeing to every request could mean we get asked to *do more* than we should while being *respected less* than we should.

You might *want* to agree to a request when you have the bandwidth to do so. When that's the case, that's the easy yes. But the challenging circumstances are packaged in the times when you want to say "yes," but doing so means you would be saying "no" to someone or something else (including yourself). Or when you want to say "no" but worry it will have repercussions against you or someone else. When requests happen in a meeting, the fact that you might have others watching can feel like its own added pressure.

We people pleasers must be everywhere because entire books have been written on the subject. One of the best I have encountered is *The Power of a Positive No: How to Say No and Still Get to Yes*, written by William Ury. Even though the book is a bit dated, the advice within it is still dead-on. By way of example, Ury retells the story of Rosa Parks who was an American black woman in the 1950s. She refused to give up her seat to a white man on a city bus and was arrested for it. Her case challenging legal segregation on public transportation went to the United States Supreme Court, where legal segregation on buses was struck down. Ury said Rosa Parks's "No on that bus was intended to protect the deeper Yes behind her No, a Yes to dignity and equality for all."[53]

Rosa Parks's "no" was far from the dead end that we often fear our own voiced "no" conveys. Your "no" doesn't need to be a dead end *at all*. In an oversimplification of what Ury teaches in his book, consider an adaptation of his "Yes! No. Yes?" model that allows you to assert your "no."

Assume you're in a meeting, and your boss asks you to take on a project with a deadline you know you can only meet *if* you sacrifice prior commitments. But starting your response by pushing back against the deadline conveys a distrust in the boss' word and makes you sound resistant to the entire project.

To avoid that outcome and come to an acceptable solution, try using the Yes! No. Yes? model like this:

Your Boss:	"Shaina, I'd like you to handle this project. We need it completed by this Thursday."
You:	"I would love to take this on! I have been looking for an opportunity just like this."
You:	"I'm committed to two other key deadlines Thursday."

Your Response Options

"I can complete this by Friday instead. Does that work?"

"I can be a second pair of eyes for another team member you assign for Thursday. Would that work?"

The clear credibility messages you convey with this approach are:

- **Yes!** You voice genuine enthusiasm for the project.
- **No.** You show commitment to other deadlines, which conveys the integrity of your follow-through.

- **Yes?** You demonstrate the leadership ability to be a window, not a door. You are doing the mental work for your boss by presenting an alternative, rather than shutting the door in their face with a "no" that goes no-where. Importantly, the alternative you offer must feel real. If it feels like a hollow gesture to your boss, you will lose credibility, not gain it. This alternative Yes? becomes your new commitment, so you want to ensure you can truly follow through.

Following the Yes! No. Yes? model conveys trust in your boss' timing and gives your boss a sense of having options while hearing your enthusiasm for the project. I have personally used this approach many times over the years, and the most common thing I learn when I use it is this: Your boss' deadline has more flexibility than originally voiced! (Of course, there are occasions where the deadline is something your boss cannot bend, but that's why you have two response options for delivering your final Yes? response.)

Challenge #3: Managing Pushback

In a perfect world, your eloquent "no" would solve all things challenging. But how many perfect-world jobs have you had? Perfection doesn't exist. But for those pretty-great jobs, it's worth the effort to grow in how you handle things like pushback from a boss or from a colleague. The challenge is keeping your ears open when you feel you're in a spiral of not being heard. Here's what I mean:

You:	"I can complete the project by Friday, okay?"
Your Boss:	"No, I really need it Thursday."
You:	"Okay, I can work with a team member you assign to get it done Thursday. How's that?"
Your Boss:	"No, I really need you to be the one who handles the whole thing. If I don't meet this deadline, my boss is going to go into this weekend's board meeting unprepared. If that happens, we'll all have hell to pay."

As you listen to the pushback, you feel frustrated that your boss doesn't seem to understand why Thursday is difficult for you, *and* you see your boss as being more self-protective with her boss rather than other-protective of you. As a result, your frustrations have caused you to shut down to what she has to say.

However, if you really listen to her, you'll realize she just gave you two key pieces of data in her pushback message. First, your boss's boss needs time with the information to feel prepared, and second, the board meeting is this weekend. This data gives you something to work with!

You:	"I see. We can solve this. Here's what I can have by Thursday so your boss can feel they have a tangible direction. I can get high-level talking points in your inbox by end-of-day Thursday to review and pass along. If your boss has those, they will have that high-level information to digest. Then, by Friday, I can get the research backup and handouts ready to go for the board meeting this weekend. How's that?"
Your Boss:	"Genius."

Now, absent your ability to get past your frustration, you may never have heard the new data to get to this creative solution. To be fair, this scenario included the fact that your boss *volunteered* additional information. But what if that doesn't happen? In this case, your job may include *mining* for the missing data.

Be kind to yourself. As my dear friend and Leadership Development Strategist Marsha Graesser often reminds me, "More than one thing can be true." It may be true that you feel frustrated and even a little worried that your boss is pushing back. It is also true that you can interview your boss in a calm manner while amid your own frustration. Again, treat your boss like data instead of like someone holding a gun to your head.

When a data researcher investigates, she uses phrasing like:

- "That's interesting. Tell me more about the *why* behind this board presentation."
- "That makes sense. Help me understand the objective for using the information."
- "I can tell the Thursday deadline is important to you. Can you tell me more about the timing?"

All types of phrasing communicate respectful curiosity rather than defensiveness or low-level panic. *That* is Kind Dynamite.

Dealing With Challenging Personalities When Managing Up

Delivering a helpful "no" to leadership and managing pushback from rational leadership is one skillset. But the next-level challenge arises when you encounter someone in a leadership role who is showing up as their most difficult. To be fair, those who show up as difficult may not be that way 24/7. In fact, when not under stress, these personalities can be likable and reasonable.

Unfortunately, stress affects the best of us. Is it in the realm of possibility that even *you* have been a difficult personality during a stressful time? Some of us commonly lack the ability to compartmentalize that stress, and it can come out sideways. Translation? That person (especially when it's your supervisor or your client) is now a difficult personality for you.

Author Mark Murphy makes an important point about the personality who seems to get away with difficult behavior. Some tolerate this person if they believe the person is a "high performer." Murphy pushes back against that characterization, noting that there is no such thing as a "high performer with a difficult personality."[54] Their challenging persona inherently makes them a low performer. Still, that person may be your boss, and you may want to make the job work.

Why Are Difficult Personalities Challenging for You?

While a person might be difficult for you to deal with, others may not feel the same. Have you ever compared "frustration notes" with a colleague and heard them say, "I don't know why you get so caught up in their drama. They aren't that bad."

Why would the same supervisor be difficult for some supervisees but not for others? Based on what clients have told me over the years, I've assembled three theories:

1. The person you find difficult reminds you of someone else who has been difficult for you in the past.
2. The person you find difficult has power over you.
3. The person you find difficult handles conflict in a way that uniquely gets to you.

There could be a fourth or even fifth reason this person is more challenging for you than for others. This is not a flaw in you. It is just how things are.

I want to push you on something. If you've compared these "frustration notes" with a colleague, are you talking to the right person? If you feel safe but are just annoyed, then comparing notes with a colleague could mean *you're* the one making things more difficult. If you can talk *to* the person you're frustrated with rather than *about* that person, you're starting from a point of respect and maturity. Look, I've been guilty of talking about a person when I knew I was rationalizing. I kidded myself that I just wanted someone else's perspective first, but in those circumstances, I was selfishly looking for an ally and potentially poisoning my colleague against the supervisor.

A Note on Difficult Personalities

If you feel psychologically or physically unsafe dealing with a difficult personality in your work environment, talk to a professional in your Human Resources group if you have one. In the most extreme cases, you may need to leave your role. Your safety cannot be compromised.

Communicating Directly with the Two Most Difficult Personalities

You know a healthy business relationship with a difficult personality when you see it. It is one where you can engage directly with the person with whom you might be struggling, even when that person is being difficult.

Many books have been written about dealing with difficult people and most of them identify seven difficult personalities or more.[55] I frequently survey teams before running trainings on dealing with difficult personalities to determine which personality types are my audience's most challenging. Even when I run these trainings internationally, the top two difficult personalities audiences identify are the Steamroller and the Know-It-All. I'll focus on these two personalities in this chapter.

The Steamroller (a.k.a., The Talented Terror)

Remember the attorney whose witness preparation I canceled when I concluded his witness was lying? That attorney came across as a Steamroller to me, even though our tense interaction was brief. I'd thankfully not encountered many Steamrollers in my life, so my understanding of this personality and my skill set in dealing with this type of person was certainly lacking.

Authors Brinkman and Kirschner call this personality "The Tank" and say this person is "on a mission, unable to slow down, pushing you around, or running right over you, the Tank has no inhibitions about ripping you apart personally. Yet the irony is... It's not personal. You just happened to get in the way."[56]

Author Mark Murphy's description of the Talented Terror category of employee fits the Steamroller's profile.[57] He calls them "emotional vampires" who suck the life out of you. They may have extreme personalities, but they may also have technical skills that keep them on the payroll. So, what defines the Steamroller's personality? Researchers note the following:

- The Steamroller must prove to themselves that their view of the world is correct. The Steamroller sees the world as black and white. There is very little gray in the Steamroller's view.
- The Steamroller's bullying typically works in the short term. They get what they want even if it means sacrificing long-term professional relationships with colleagues.
- The Steamroller doesn't respect those who back down, even though their behavior seems to communicate that they want you to do exactly that. If you know anything about the Steamroller's closest friends, you can often see a pattern

of stronger personalities in the Steamroller's sphere, especially ones who will not back down to the Steamroller.

What Not to Do When Encountering the Steamroller

Anytime someone in our path is extreme, it's tempting to become extreme in our own behavior and become a Steamroller ourselves, counterattacking with anger. It might feel justified, after all. On the other extreme, you might want to back away. The last thing you want to do is to get flattened by the Steamroller.

What To Do When Encountering the Steamroller

Fortunately, there are two key ways to effectively deal with the Steamroller. Both are effective, even if they feel counterintuitive.

First, set a realistic goal for dealing with the Steamroller. Brinkman and Kirschner offer wise advice on this front. They advise being alert to the fact that you will not change the Steamroller's personality. You will also not persuade the Steamroller to see the gray in the black-and-white world where the Steamroller lives. So, what is your goal when working with a Steamroller? Simply to command respect in the short term. It may take a longer path to achieve more specific work goals with the Steamroller.

Second, I recommend following four specific steps outlined by Brinkman and Kirschner when working with the Steamroller: [58]

1. Stand your ground and maintain steady eye contact. The Steamroller may address you in an intimidating manner, and your nonverbal behavior needs to show calm confidence.
2. Give the Steamroller time to run out of steam.
3. Interrupt the attack once you feel the Steamroller is winding down. You will need to be efficient with your words. It wouldn't hurt to lodge in a Curiosity Filter statement.
4. Present the bottom line of your point.

Let's assume your interaction with the Steamroller begins with their misplaced belief that you failed to do a task well that an important client needed. Here's what your conversation will look like following Brinkman and Kirschner's four steps:

Steamroller:	"I can't believe how badly you botched this incredibly simple assignment for our most important client! They had an urgent problem. They needed an answer within the hour. I counted on you to solve it."
Steamroller:	"How did I ever trust that you would be able to handle this job? My twelve-year-old could have done a better job than you did."
You:	[Maintain steady eye contact.]
	"It turns out your trust was well-placed. The client didn't get one important thing. She got two."
You:	"I came up with two new ways to solve their problem. The plan with options is already in the client's inbox and yours."

These four steps are great when you have them in hand. At first, you may feel some struggle executing them. But have them ready. The one thing you can count on with the Steamroller is predictability. You will get more opportunities to practice. Stick with it. You'll get better with time.

The Know-It-All (a.k.a., The Overconfident, Sometimes Competent-Sometimes-Incompetent Personality)

At first glance, the Know-It-All can seem more reasonable than the Steamroller since they're not a yeller. But the irony about the Know-It-All is that they share some things in common with the Steamroller. The Know-It-All still wants control, just like the Steamroller. Because they don't yell, their personality seems less overtly aggressive even though their firm belief in the superiority of knowledge is an aggressive trait.

Brinkman and Kirschner describe this personality well. According to them, "Know-It-Alls control people and events by dominating the conversation with lengthy, imperious arguments, and they eliminate opposition by finding flaws and weaknesses to discredit other points of view."[59] The irony is the Know-It-All doesn't know much about their own personality and drives.

It is a given that the Know-It-All truly wants admiration and acknowledgement of his or her intellectual prowess. The Know-It-All also lacks the ability to understand their "superior" knowledge comes only from partial information, rather than full awareness. Most Know-It-Alls live quite comfortably in the world of half-knowledge and are willing to add new, unproven knowledge to that half-wisdom.

What Not to Do When Encountering the Know-It-All

The reality of the Know-It-All is that they can talk and talk — and then talk some more. That can be more than annoying. It can inspire you to try to out-talk the person and correct them with your knowledge. Sound familiar? Keep this in mind: The Know-It-All may actually Know-It-Some. You may find this personality's proclamations so outlandish that you want to dismiss this person altogether, but at second glance, this person may add some value. Granted, mining for that value may be exhausting. You may want to move on. Consider ways to be more discerning in the following section.

What To Do When Encountering the Know-It-All

As with the Steamroller, there are two positive ways to deal with the Know-It-All that you may not have tried because they can be counterintuitive.

First, set a realistic goal for dealing with the Know-It-All. You won't talk the Know-It-All out of their narcissistic beliefs in their "superior" knowledge. So, what is realistic with this difficult personality? In the professional setting, you may have two audiences: the Know-It-All and others within earshot of your encounter, especially if you're in a meeting. Your goal with the Know-It-All is to get her to consider alternative views. Your goal with your "earshot audience" is to help educate them on additional (or corrected) information. No matter what, you do not want to shame the Know-It-All in the process.

Second, I recommend following these five steps developed by Brinkman and Kirschner when working with the Know-It-All: [60]

1. Listen intently to the Know-It-All for whatever information might be accurate.
2. Verbally acknowledge the information you know to be accurate from what the Know-It-All just said.
3. Question the inaccuracies firmly and with a tone of genuine curiosity.
4. Present your facts as "alternatives," and do so with a respectful tone.
5. If possible, move on to another issue. The Know-It-All is often eager to stay on the same point and pontificate.

Assume the Know-It-All wants your organization to adopt a new policy based on partial information. Use Brinkman and Kirschner's steps to form your strong starting point:

Know-It-All: "I doubt you know this, but research shows that we will double our sales if we advertise on [outdated social media platform] because most young consumers get their news on fashion trends from this particular platform."

You: "I like where you're headed. You're right that social media is where young consumers learn fashion trends."

You: "Do you think the platform you're referring to has the latest demographic information about who is using it the most?"

You: "Perhaps this platform was the "it platform" for young consumers a while back, but the new addition of other platforms is edging out their market share with young consumers. What if we looked at the platform you mentioned and then threw in a look at the other platforms to compare? I know you have a good statistical tool to analyze that information."

After getting the Know-It-All's buy-in to do a statistical comparison, say, "By the way, could you show me the latest software you use for the statistical analysis? My chi-square skills are a little, well, square." Then, if possible, move on to another issue. The Know-It-All is often eager to stay on the same point and pontificate.

Remember, the Know-It-All deeply craves admiration. There is no better strategy than to ask the Know-It-All to teach you something you genuinely want to know.

Your Verbal Power Will Serve You During the Challenges

As daunting as managing up or as challenging as difficult encounters can be, they are inevitable. You can waste your time bemoaning that fact, or you can take pushback and difficult personalities head-on. Remember what brought you to your role in your organization. You have been chosen for this job for good reason. Your voice is worth amplifying. Use your independent thinking to chart a future goal using Kind Dynamite. You do *not* need to allow pushback and difficult personalities to define your methods. Use your verbal power. You will respect yourself more and that is reason enough to assert as effectively as possible.

CHAPTER 9

PowerPoint Persuasion in Meetings

If you create a PowerPoint slide to be self-explanatory without you, you just create a lousy slide. (Oh, and you just made yourself irrelevant at the same time.)

A Fortune 50 technology company recently asked me to make a presentation to their legal team about persuasive presentations and public speaking. I knew I wanted to touch on PowerPoint tips, so I asked the organizer if one of the lawyers would be willing to share an actual slide deck they'd created in advance so that I could critique it as part of the presentation. One of them quickly (and courageously) complied.

The minute the deck hit my inbox, I knew it was *bad*. The information in the slides was smart and important. Unfortunately, it was buried by the layout and the volume of material included. I knew these issues would tank its effectiveness with the audience, so I reworked the slides to demonstrate how much better they could be.

The day of the presentation arrived, and I logged in to the online platform to address the audience. The first thing I said was, "Did you know there's a terrific program for creating documents called Word? This PowerPoint deck has so many words that it is masquerading as a Word document. We're going to fix that."

Despite my criticisms of the misuses of PowerPoint slides (and I have *many*), I'm pro-PowerPoint! I create and use slides all the time in meetings and in presentations. But bad PowerPoint decks are like drinking too much vodka. A little might be great, and a lot will put you to sleep (or worse).

If you're like me, you've been subjected to terrible PowerPoint decks over the years. Somehow, bad decks beget bad decks. The more we see bad examples, the more we seem to replicate them. (By the way, I'll keep referring to PowerPoint in this chapter since it is my go-to tool, but the techniques I describe here apply equally to any presentation software of your choice.)

It turns out, poor PowerPoints are more than simply annoying to the viewer. Solid research finds that bad PowerPoint slides *actually decrease* an audience's learning.[61] Despite your good intentions, you just might be hurting your audience (and your credibility) if your slides commit the four sins so many decks do.

Sin #1: Too Much Text

Take a look at this slide. It comes from a template presentation provided through PowerPoint:

Image 3: Too Much Text on a Slide

I doubt I need to show you many examples of this sin since you've likely been subjected to more text-heavy slides than you care to count. The question is, have you subjected your meeting attendees to the same?

Look, I get it. When I ask clients about their instincts to throw so much text on their slides, their answers commonly fall into one of three common categories:

Category#1: "I want to ensure the slide reinforces what I'm saying."

Newsflash — your meeting attendees can read. If all you do is read your slide aloud *to them*, you will insult your audience's intelligence and simultaneously put them to sleep.

Of all the slide atrocities, the presence of bullet points and too much text is where the neuroscience research finds the greatest fall-off in learning. In your viewer's brain, your slide's content competes with your verbal point. Are you also verbalizing additional information when you flash up a text-heavy slide? Most of us do. If so, you lose because your attendees pay less attention to you than to your slide.

Category #2: "I have been asked to provide a handout of my slides."

Are you certain? In most cases, you've been asked to provide a handout of your *content*. That is *not* the same as being asked to provide a copy of your slides for all attendees.

Here's the spoiler: When you need to provide a handout, your *worst-case* scenario is to force your PowerPoint slides to double as a presentation and as a takeaway document. When I'm asked to provide a handout, I create a Word document that summarizes my content. Does it take extra work? Yes. Does it make my PowerPoint deck stay truer to being a persuasive presentation device? Yes.

Category#3: "I want to ensure I don't lose my place."

There it is. You made your slides double as *your* speaking script, and you just rationalized making them text-heavy for the attendees' sake when, in fact, you made them text-heavy for yourself. I'll grant you this — it's clever. It even sounds altruistic. But weren't you *just* in another meeting where someone bored you to (invisible) tears with *their* text-heavy slides? Don't forget that experience! Don't commit the same sin.

The Better Way

I have good news for you. There is a way to revise a text-heavy slide to preserve the mnemonic crutch you need as a speaker and to ensure you impart reinforcing wisdom to your viewer.

Look at this improved variation on the bad slide:

Image 4: An Improved Slide to Combat Too Much Text

You have no doubt noticed that this version of the slide needs a presenter to provide the context and relevant information. That is a sign of an *excellent* slide. The visual nature of the slide offers the audience a chance to mentally engage, and it provides you a mnemonic reminder of your key point.

If you're using Zoom or some other videoconferencing tool, you can privately display your presentation notes to guide your talking points. But do yourself a big favor, and don't write your notes out word for word. That will diminish your dynamism and credibility.

Image 5: *How to Protect Your Speaker Notes in the Notes View*

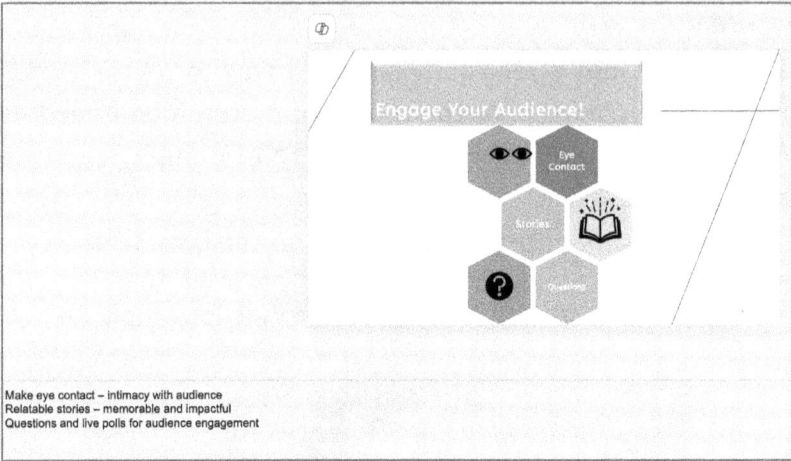

Sin #2: Letting the Viewer Get Ahead of You

Any time you have more than one point on a slide (visual or otherwise), you can be certain that the audience will out-pace your coverage of anything that comes after the first point. Take this slide for example:

Image 6: *Failing to Animate Your Text as You Speak*

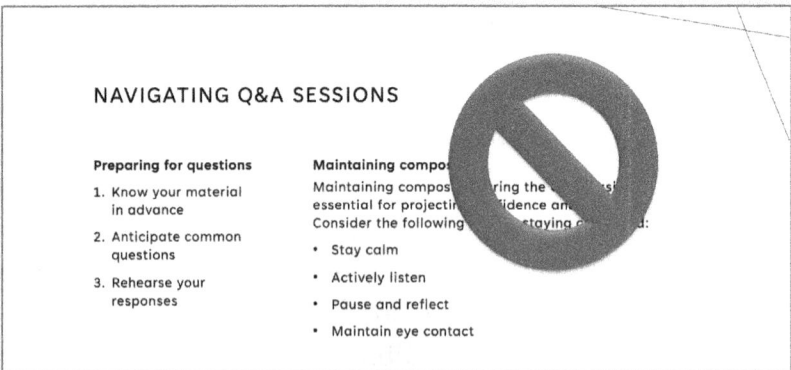

I'm floored any time a presenter thinks the viewer will patiently wait to read the next point or look at the next chart until the presenter verbally gets to that point. Your viewer will *not* wait for you. You don't wait when you're the viewer.

When your audience is reading ahead, you've lost control of where they're looking, and you just lost the neuro-competition. Your audience's brain power is focused on reading your slide, not on listening to you, which means you're not effectively teaching your points.

The Better Ways

There are two easy ways to keep control of the pace at which your colleagues view your points. The first way is to only include one point per slide.

Image 7: Controlling the Pace of the Viewer's View

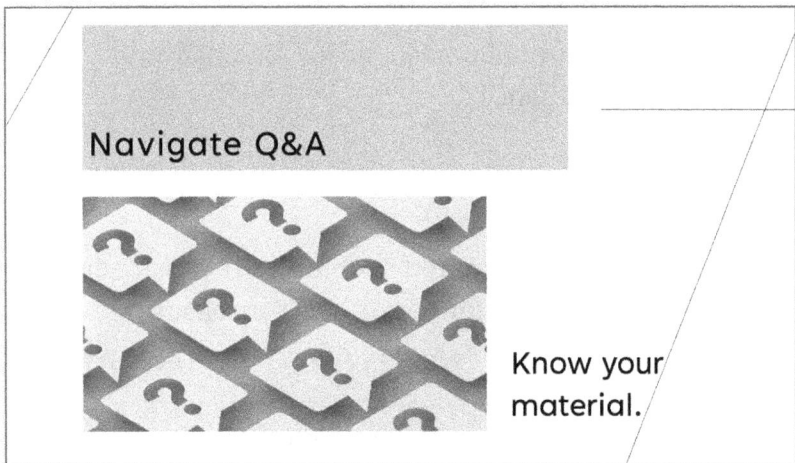

The second way is to use the animation feature in your presentation platform. You can then click your mouse the moment *you're* ready to cover the next point rather than cede that premature control to your viewer. The animation feature in PowerPoint is highly intuitive as it is in other presentation platforms. Using PowerPoint as an example, you can find detailed directions on Microsoft's support page by searching "animate text or objects" using the search bar at the top of the page.

Sin #3: Leaving Expired Slides on The Screen

When you finish your point on a slide, what do you do until you're ready to make your next point? Do you leave the slide on the screen until you click to the next one? Or, if you have only one slide to show, do you leave it up until you move to something else, like a whiteboard function? You may have moved on, but your viewer might still be scrutinizing the slide, either for content or out of sheer boredom. At this point, your slide has expired like bad milk, and it distracts your audience.

The Better Ways

Rather than leave an expired slide on your screen, create a sense of "the current" for your viewer by ensuring you remove the slide as soon as you're done. There are two ways to do this.

The first way to keep your audience in sync with what you're currently saying is to use a little-known keystroke in PowerPoint that makes the screen blank without closing your presentation. When in presentation mode, hit the

B key on your keyboard if you want the screen to go black until you're ready for your next slide. Then, hit the *B* key again when you want to reveal your deck. If you prefer to show a white screen, use the *W* key.

The second way to keep your audience from fixating on an expired PowerPoint slide is to take down the deck altogether when you're completely done. Too often, we get engaged in the rest of the meeting and forget we no longer need the deck to stay up. Stop sharing your screen!

Sin #4: Crowding Out the Main Visual Aid (You)

When you share your screen to display a presentation deck in the virtual session, most platforms currently default to making the slide show take up most of the real estate on the viewer's screen. This is truly unfortunate because *you* should be the main visual aid. Before you share your presentation or document, the screen typically looks like the one shown in Image 8.

Image 8: The Default View of Your Screen
Before Sharing a Presentation

Then, once you share your screen, the default view looks like Image 9. in most applications. In any and all presentations, the presenter should be the main visual aid; however, in this view, the presenter is smaller, and the shared document dominates.

Image 9: *The Default View of Your Shared Screen After Sharing a Presentation*

I analogize this default to the bad habit many audiovisual teams have of turning down the house lights in a conference room when you're presenting live to an audience. Doing this means you just became a literal shadow while your presentation deck became the main attraction!

The Better Ways

There are two ways to ensure your presence isn't diminished during a virtual meeting. The first way requires easy cooperation from your viewers while you give them three simple directions. Using Zoom as an example, share your presentation and then instruct your viewers to complete the following steps:

1. Choose gallery side view. (If you're not using Zoom, you'll need to find these settings within that application. If your chosen videoconferencing application doesn't offer this view, you may want to find one that does.)

Image 10: *Step One to Fix the Imbalance Ratio*

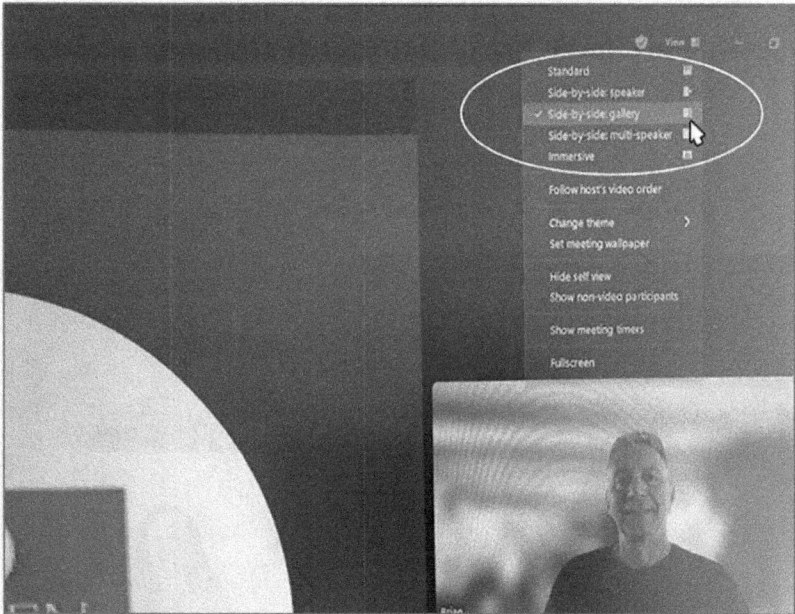

2. Hover your cursor over the vertical line dividing the slide from the gallery side view. In Zoom, a double-sided arrow appears as you see in Image 11.

Image 11: *Step Two to Fix the Imbalance Ratio*

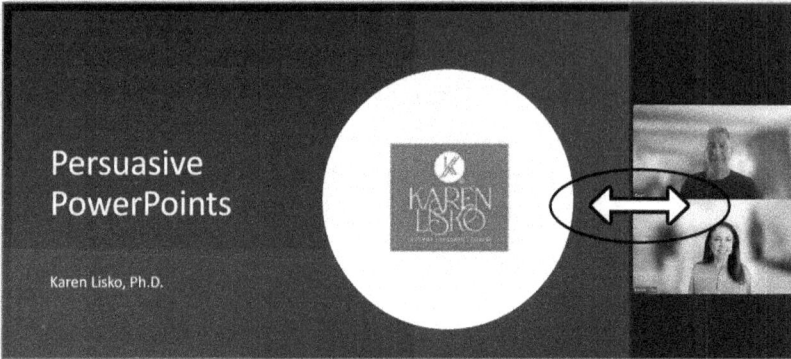

3. Slide the vertical line to the left until you've enlarged the gallery view of the presenter and meeting participants and shrunk the slide to a still-legible size.

Image 12: *Step Three to Fix the Imbalance Ratio*

Now, the imbalance is gone, and the presenter or presenters are more prominent in the virtual presentation!

The second way requires no work from your viewers. You'll simply need to share your screen at times, stop sharing it when you don't need a given slide, and reshare your screen again when you do. Doing this may feel disjointed, but it gives your viewers some variety. I've seen this simple approach refresh viewers' attention simply because the size of the gallery changes when sharing and unsharing a presentation.

Lead Others Through Your PowerPoint Presentation

Done well, you can more persuasively use a presentation deck when you're inclined to teach that way. You also have the power to influence others about the more persuasive ways to create and use PowerPoint slides. If you're mindful of the better ways to create slides and share them, your meeting attendees will notice your approach. Even more optimistically, they just may follow your lead when creating their own decks.

Kind Dynamite means you're asserting the right way to present with a deck while kindly leading through your own example. Chapter 10 will offer additional ways to keep your virtual meetings more engaging. Your credibility will benefit, and your colleagues will appreciate you for it!

Virtual Persuasion in Your Online Meeting

Persuasion changes when your meeting
is online, and your delivery does too.

Humanity craves connection, both professionally and personally. When the world pandemic of 2020 put us into lockdown, things changed and fast. But, in its isolation, locked-down humanity continued to crave connectivity. If you were in the professional workforce during that time, you probably entered the Zoom Era (or choose your favorite platform — Microsoft Teams, Google Meet, Cisco Webex, the list goes on).

In March 2020, my boss asked me to quickly create a training for our attorneys and business professionals on how to communicate effectively via Zoom. I said, "Sure!" and then set to work figuring out what the hell Zoom was. I was literally only five minutes ahead of everyone else with my virtual communication knowledge, but figure it out I did!

What was foreign at that time has now become commonplace in the business world. So much so that we quickly entered what I call the Zoom Fatigue Era. It is so real that there is now a scale for it (and, of course, as a social scientist, I'm all over it). Aptly naming it the Zoom Exhaustion and Fatigue Scale, researchers have identified the many ways we become more tired when on Zoom compared with attending a meeting in person.[62] But guess which gender gets fatigued more frequently? That's right. Women.

Great. One more thing to feel tired about.

Here's what's fascinating: The *reason* women experience more frequent fatigue tracks precisely with what I addressed in Chapter 6. Women have the superpower of being more attuned to nonverbal language than men. We read nonverbal cues on Zoom more often. We sometimes suffer more from "mirror anxiety" as a result of monitoring our own images on Zoom, and we can tire from being physically restrained within our Zoom "box." As a result, our Zoom experience is more exhausting than men's.[63]

Now, you may wonder, why would I start this chapter on such a downer? It turns out women have an immense opportunity to be more effective because so many others just aren't thinking about ways to combat this fatigue. This chapter is about more than battling that fatigue. It's about creating a virtual experience that is just as persuasive as an in-person one. Get five minutes ahead of everyone else, and you'll be a meeting standout.

Move Your Virtual Meetings from Monologue to Dialogue

Because attention spans can wane more quickly in the virtual environment, we have an opportunity and a mandate to make meetings more interactive, whether we are running the entire discussion or just a segment. *Do not* fall into the trap of "following the (meeting) leader" when that leader's approach is predictable and monologic.

(Okay, I must admit I got lucky when I wrote the word "monologic." It turns out it's really a word relating to monologues! Feel free to borrow it.)

Start With the End in Mind

In Chapter 2, we looked at thin-slice research that finds people form impressions of us within mere seconds. Even if you've landed in virtual meetings with the same participants in the past, use those first few seconds to your benefit. Start with the end of the meeting in mind and pull your meeting participants immediately into the discussion.

Considering the speed with which virtual platforms and apps are innovating tools for meetings, it's likely even more are being invented as I write this paragraph. Therefore, take these next few examples as purely that — examples. Take care of your meeting attendees by keeping up with and researching new tools. The options will certainly grow in our virtual world.

Use a Whiteboard to Organize Goals and Decisions

Nothing focuses a discussion more than talking about the decisions that need to be made by the time the meeting ends. Virtual platforms have whiteboards that allow you, as the discussion leader, to write up and organize the list of items. This visual list:

1. Pulls in your participants' sense of ownership in the meeting.
2. Disciplines the flow of discussion.
3. Creates accountability to revisit the list of action items at the meeting's end.

Don't limit yourself to using the whiteboard simply to create the "decision list" within the meeting. Also, use another area of the whiteboard during the meeting to list action items the team needs to own after the meeting ends.

Once you become conversant with a good whiteboard tool, you can use it for other visuals, importing documents, and blessedly, to combat Zoom Fatigue. Think about it. By using a whiteboard, you are pulling your team away from the self-mirroring gallery view that dominates so many virtual meetings. Your visual learners will love it, and it will help provide a break from the static gallery view.

Hold Yourself Accountable with a Timed Agenda

What meeting ever sticks to the schedule? If your team is willing to try it, use the timed agenda that is often so easily accessible in video platforms. Giving your team a paced agenda gives them predictability and momentum. You might just find they stay more engaged as a result. I have most frequently used the timer-agenda app by BlueSky, and I recommend giving it a try.

Pace the Dialogue

When you single-handedly control the agenda in the virtual setting, you have the opportunity and responsibility *to do something different* than what most meeting leaders do, and that is to treat the virtual medium like in-person meetings. This is a big mistake for two reasons.

First, regardless of whether they're conducted in person or virtually, most meetings are ineffective "update strings," focusing on a topic-by-topic briefing rather than being action-oriented. You've been in those meetings. When the donuts are the highlight of the hour, you know you're in trouble.

Meetings are too rich an opportunity for in-the-moment discussion and debate with the bright minds hired to think. Use your meetings to make decisions and to schedule action, not to rattle off a list of updates. For updates, use email instead.

Second, the virtual medium has so many tools to keep the dialogue lively and decision-focused. Consider four specific approaches to keep the virtual meeting interactive:

1. Use Live Polling
2. Pose Real Questions, Not Rhetorical Ones
3. Facilitate Intentional Disagreement
4. Cameo Your Guest Appearances

It's important to pace your use of these approaches. Intersperse these tools at regular intervals to mitigate Zoom Fatigue and your team will thank you. If you aren't the one running the meeting, use your Kind Dynamite assertiveness to suggest these tools or use them in your portion of the meeting.

Interactive Approach #1: Use Live Polling

In the virtual setting, you have a genuine opportunity to engage the attendees seated in front of their keyboards (in other words, everyone). If you intersperse polling questions throughout your meeting with your attendees so they can weigh in either with opinions or on quiz questions, you will immediately engage their focus. Could you ask these questions aloud? Sure. But, asking polling questions *in addition to* verbal questions provides variety *and* anonymity. It can also be fun for your attendees. Imagine that. The words *fun* and *meetings* aren't frequent companions!

Polling platforms are easy to learn (if you're creating the questions and if you're taking the polls) and are completely customizable. While options come with video platforms like Zoom or Microsoft Teams, the one I currently use the most is an external program called Slido.[64] I use it to embed questions either within a PowerPoint deck or I can access it as a stand-alone feature while using Zoom. (As with other technology, by the time you finish reading this paragraph, more polling options are certain to have entered the market!)

Two of the most common ways you can use polling include testing attendees' knowledge and getting their input.

When polling to test your attendees' knowledge, your goal is to engage your audience without shaming them if they don't get the answer right. Consider this quiz question I commonly use: Most people speak at a rate of 140 words per minute. How many words per minute do you think most people can hear?

Image 13: *A Sample Multiple-Choice Quiz Question*

Most people speak at a rate of 140 words per minutes. How many words per minute do you think most people can hear?

- **70 words per minute**

- **120 words per minute**

- **240 words per minute**

- **300 words per minute**

Most people get this question wrong — which is partly the point. If you use polling for obvious answers, it can bore your attendees. Your polling platform then reveals the correct answer: 300 words per minute.

Image 14: *A Sample Answer to the*
Multiple-Choice Quiz Question

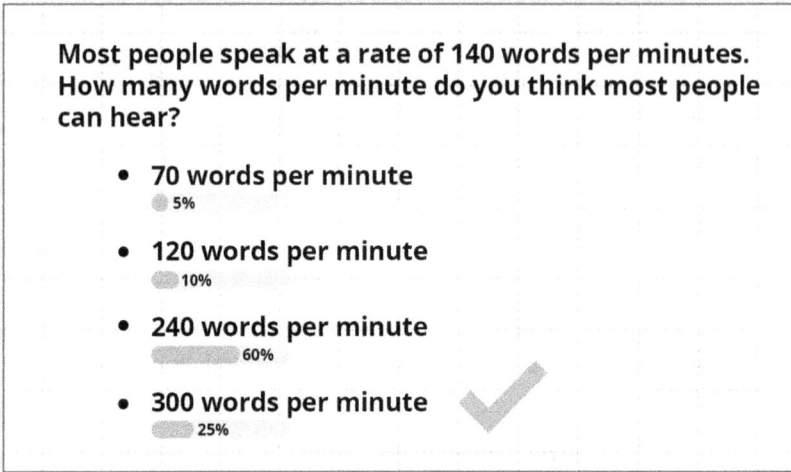

Most people speak at a rate of 140 words per minutes. How many words per minute do you think most people can hear?

- **70 words per minute**
  5%

- **120 words per minute**
  10%

- **240 words per minute**
  60%

- **300 words per minute** ✔
  25%

Then, you can have a live discussion of the answer's implications. For this topic, I explain that the reality that people can absorb up to three hundred words per minute means their minds can wander and come back to you as the speaker while *you're still on the same point!* As a result, strong speakers should talk at a conversational, slightly faster pace and embed strategic pausing to break things up and draw attention to their next sentence.

If you're polling to gather your attendees' input, consider what you might ask in an open-ended way to collect ideas. My favorite feature is the "word cloud" because it enables everyone to enter their own wording while also showcasing the most common answers.

Assume you want to ask your group about preferences for a holiday celebration. You could ask: Within our budget, we have options for an offsite gathering. What would your ideal group celebration include?

Image 15: *A Sample Open-Ended Question*

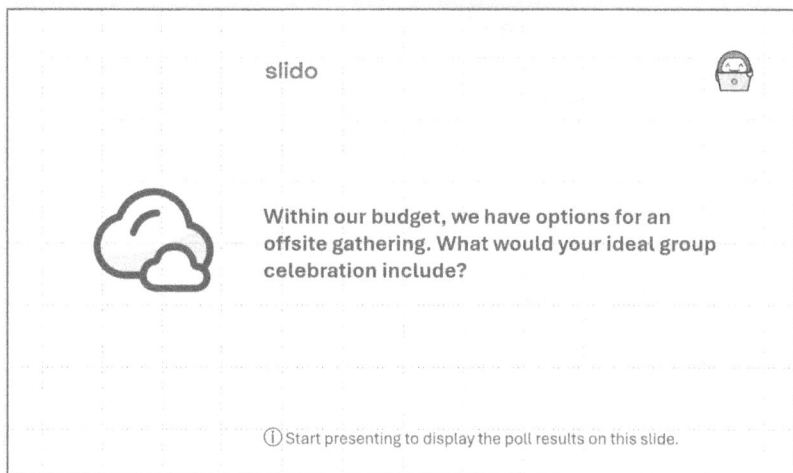

Attendees' responses can be both useful and clever. You have given free rein to anonymous input and created *a unique way* for your meeting attendees to use their collective voice. The group's open-ended responses will start to populate the screen as they enter their responses.

Interactive Approach #2: Pose Real Questions, Not Rhetorical Ones

I don't know about you, but most of the virtual meetings I attend seem to devolve quickly to having less interaction than the live meetings I sit through — at least when the leader fails to plan for engagement. The virtual setting can create a passive atmosphere for attendees if you don't actively bring them into the conversation. This quietude seems especially prevalent among more junior employees. Set the tone as the leader by ensuring you pose questions with an expectation that someone (or several someones) will respond. Three plans can help you succeed at creating greater interaction (see Image 16).

Image 16: *Three Question-Related Plans for Creating Interaction*

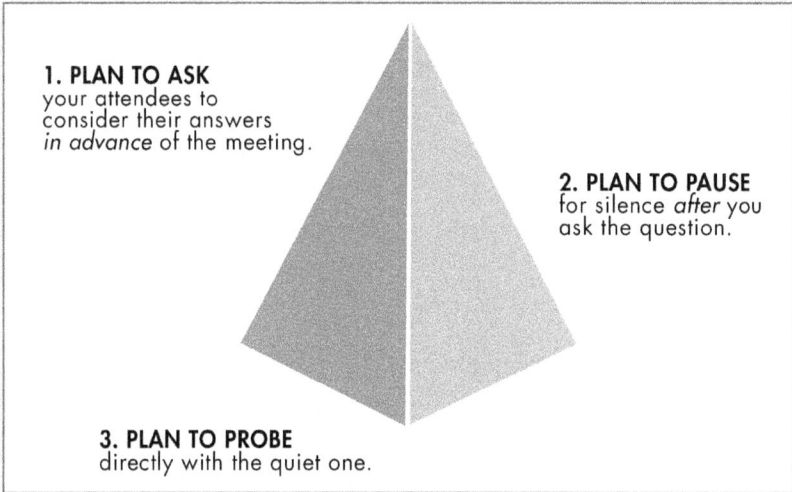

1. PLAN TO ASK your attendees to consider their answers *in advance* of the meeting.

2. PLAN TO PAUSE for silence *after* you ask the question.

3. PLAN TO PROBE directly with the quiet one.

Plan Element #1: Plan to ask your attendees to consider their answers in advance.

There is some abject unfairness when *you* know the questions you plan to ask your meeting attendees, but *they* don't. I get it — there may be exceptions where you don't want them to have a meeting question in their back pocket to think about. But ask yourself this: If there is no good reason to hold back on the questions in advance, why not let your attendees ponder their responses in advance too? (Of course, divulging questions before the meeting requires you to think through your questions in advance!)

In fact, you may just get more engagement in the meeting with that advance step. But — and this is a big but — do not allow attendees to engage in an advance sidebar conversation with you regarding their responses. That violates the no-unfair-meetings-before-the-meeting rule.

Plan Element #2: Plan to pause for silence after you ask the question.

Anytime you ask a question — planned or not — ask yourself this: Have I "saved the silence" by answering my own question? You know what I mean because you've seen it repeatedly in meetings. A presenter or leader asks a question, a few (to several) beats of silence ensue, and then the presenter panics and answers the question themself. I call this "pause panic" because that is exactly why a person converts a genuine question into a rhetorical one. As questioners, we don't like silence. We see it as failure, either on our part so we "question the question" or on the listener's part for failing to jump in to save the silence.

Guess what? When you posed a question, you knew it was coming. Most of the time, the listener did not. The silence just might be your audience pondering the question. Let the silence happen. Someone will answer. How do I know? Because I test this theory every time I ask a question in a meeting or a presentation. 100 percent of the time, someone responds.

They might respond because they had time to ponder their answer, and my silence gave them the space to speak up. They also might do it out of pity to break the "pause panic." I have learned not to care about their motivation.

The silence is worth it because the demonstration of patience teaches your attendees that you're genuinely interested in hearing their voices in response.

Plan Element #3: Plan to probe directly with the quiet one.

Nearly every time I call on a meeting attendee who has *not* volunteered to speak, I come away impressed. The quiet attendees are not necessarily checked out, nor are they silently sitting in judgment of you, much as your own self-doubt may wonder. (Okay, sometimes there is judgment. We are humans, after all.) The point is that we too readily read into the silence as a negative, and worse, we often skip over the person who stays mute.

Besides leading meetings, I run focus groups for a living. I question attendees by Zoom all the time in my work, and I have learned that the quiet ones can surprise you with their spoken depth and logic. Too often, we let the talkative volunteers dominate the meeting. Some people's *personalities* cause them to hang back, but they still add great value through their comments when you call on them. Additionally, some people's *cultures* cause them to wait to be called on out of respect for your authority.

When you do call on the quiet one, take great care to use a tone of curiosity rather than a tone of sarcasm when addressing their silence. The quiet one isn't fragile, but you won't earn anyone's respect if you chide the person for not speaking up. Kind Dynamite is about a respectful tone and assertiveness when calling on someone who has not volunteered. One of my favorite respectful nudges is to phrase my question like, "Xavier, what's on your mind about this?" The quiet one always has something on their mind.

Interactive Approach #3: Facilitate
Intentional Disagreement

Using a Kind Dynamite approach means you can create a safe and animated environment for debate. One of my favorite studies confirmed that a predominant tone of co-operation creates *worse* decisions when you know there is controversy around a topic.[65] Set clear and overt meeting rules for the debate you want to foster a discussion with differing opinions. Borrowing from Patrick Lencioni, who wrote *Death by Meeting*, the meeting rules I urge leaders to publish and "virtually laminate" for every meeting are noted in Image 17.[66][67]

Image 17: *The Six Meeting Rules That Encourage Productive Friction*

The Six Meeting Rules That Encourage "Productive Friction"

1. **Everyone** puts their perspectives on the table.
2. **Everyone** supports the final decision.
3. **Anyone** "mines" for diverse opinions (conflict).
4. **Anyone** interrupts tension with reminder of importance.
5. **No one** prevents diverse opinions (conflict) from being fleshed out.
6. **No one** "stomps out virtually" or mentally shuts down during the meeting.

Patrick Lencioni

Interactive Approach #4: Cameo Your Guest Appearances

When the 2020 pandemic hit, and I was asked to train lawyers on effective ways to show up in virtual meetings from their home offices, I decided to address the virtual backgrounds people used in those early days. I recruited two attorneys in leadership at the law firm to pop into my presentation. I knew from prior interactions that the two attorneys I'd invited sat in front of starkly different backgrounds when they appeared in meetings from their home offices.

One of the attorneys sat in front of an elegant, paneled wall you might expect to see behind a senior attorney. The other equally senior and smart attorney sat in front of a hodgepodge of bobble-headed collectibles. By showcasing them live (and as a surprise to the meeting attendees) during my presentation, we added entertainment value and good-natured ribbing of their chosen styles.

Days after that meeting, attendees still mentioned that standout portion of my presentation. The beauty of it was how little work it took to include our senior staff. Persuasion happens through the unexpected, and guest appearances from senior members of our team fit the bill! In that setting, I simply brought each attorney's live camera view into the meeting. But if you want to show a guest star *within* a prepared slide, PowerPoint and other presentation software have a "cameo" feature you can use quite easily. When you present your slides, your image (or the guest star's image) will appear in the lower right corner of the screen, as shown in Image 18.

Image 18: A View of a Live Cameo Within Your Slide

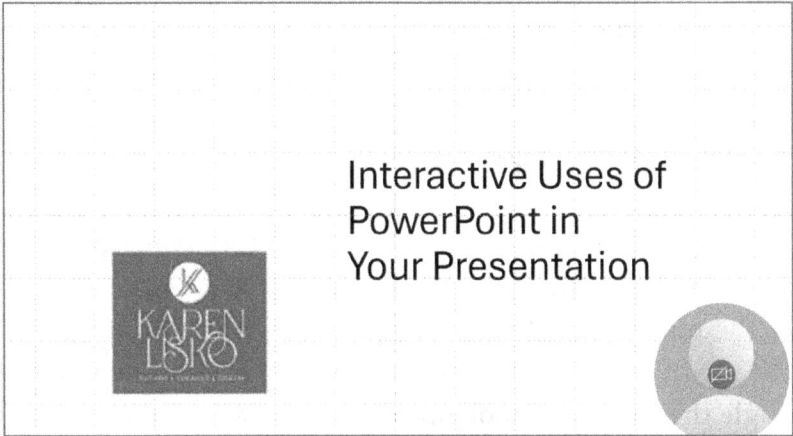

This approach allows the live guest star to narrate the slide that appears on the screen. It adds variety to whoever is speaking, and it's impactful. The brevity of the cameo feature also takes pressure off your guest's appearance on the screen. Let that person make a brief, impromptu, on-camera cameo, and you're likely to get a more willing "yes" from the busy person you want to appear in your meeting.

Upgrade Your Equipment in Three Important Ways

You prepare for your meeting. You think about your objectives. You organize your remarks. You turn on your equipment. And the visual image you project is lackluster. Why go to so much effort only to tolerate a bad equipment setup in your virtual meetings?

We're still friends, yes? You read the great evidence I provided about the importance of nonverbal cues in

Chapter 6. Take it to heart with regards to your virtual set-up and do some simple equipment upgrades that yield big dividends in your nonverbal credibility.

Upgrade #1: The Right Camera

Most computer cameras are in exactly the wrong position to give your audience the best view of you. They're either at the top of your monitor looking down on you or are on the top of your laptop screen where you might unwittingly angle the camera to look up your nose. Let's face it: neither angle is a good look.

The ideal angle is straight into the screen at eye level so you can make terrific eye contact with those you're looking at across the pixelation. That would mean having a camera *in* your screen — which is certainly on the horizon invention-wise. Until then, there are terrific work-arounds. Several external cameras hang into the middle of your screen, either from above or from below. The version I most frequently recommend is the HUE camera.[68]

Image 19: The HUE Camera

The camera is small, but it does take time to adjust to looking at your screen with a camera dangling right in the middle. I analogize it to seeing a squashed bug on your windshield as you drive. You notice it at first, and then you quickly work around it. The benefits of this adaptation are well worth it. Those with whom you interact virtually will feel you're looking directly at them. In addition, if you want to have notes on your screen as you speak, you can refer to them without looking down.

Upgrade #2: The Right Lighting

No camera will show you in your best light if your best light is, well, too dim. Consider these rules of thumb from the professionals:

- If you have a window in your workspace, try to position your computer in front of the window to light your face. If the window is behind you, it can cast your face in shadow. If the window must be behind you, use blinds or curtains to block the light.
- Light your face with artificial light if natural light is not quite enough (and natural light is rarely enough). The best type of light is diffused light, which is a softer, filtered light. Light from behind a lampshade is an example of diffused light, but you'll likely need something more direct on your face in an online setting. Shop around for something that is attachable to a computer monitor. Ring lights are *not* examples of diffuse light, and they create their own challenges when reflected in the lenses of eyeglasses in Zoom meetings.

- If you can also have diffuse light on your shoulders, you will enhance your image on screen, but the most important lighting in a pinch is light directly facing you.

Upgrade #3: The Right Audio

You can check the box for *adequate* audio by using your computer microphone, but they can also catch ambient noise and make you sound as if you have an echo in your voice. If you want your voice to be clear, use wired or wireless earbuds with a built-in microphone.

Adjust Your Delivery Style for the Virtual Environment

Chapter 6 covered delivery elements in detail, but the virtual environment demands some minor variation on that advice.

Express Greater Energy

Because you pixelate across your screen to your colleague's screen, your presence becomes somewhat muted in comparison to in-person interactions. Bear in mind the essence of Kind Dynamite. Dynamism is the "credibility constellation" that sets you apart from other passable speakers. You will need to amplify your dynamism in the virtual setting to an extent that may feel somewhat exaggerated to you. I do a significant number of presentations from my home office, and I *still* feel exaggerated when I "up" my dynamism to the right level for this setting!

The Three Virtual Vocal Cues That Matter

There are three vocal cues you should capitalize on in the virtual setting to immediately sound more compelling:

1. **Pause** for impact.
2. Increase your **volume** to project energy.
3. Keep your **pace** slightly faster and conversational.

Image 20: The Three Important Virtual Vocal Cues

The Five Virtual Visual Cues That Make You More Compelling

Given the prominence of your face (and everyone else's) on virtual platforms, your nonverbal cues are more noticeable than when you're in a large conference room. Of all the visual cues outlined in Chapter 6, know that these five are most important:

1. Smile whenever possible to convey warmth.
2. Ensure your face is expressive.
3. Keep your hands away from your face and hair.
4. Show facial reactions when listening.
5. Elevate your hand gestures to be seen.

Image 21: *The Five Important Virtual Visual Cues*

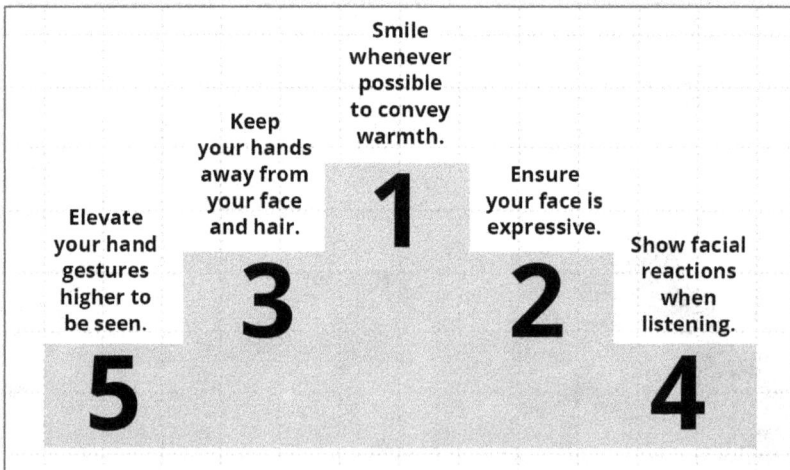

Bring Your Three-Dimensional Self to the Screen

Virtual communication is its own medium, to be sure. But as you have undoubtedly recognized, persuasive communication in this setting significantly overlaps in-person communication.

Two key distinctions are endemic to virtual persuasion. First, the reality of Zoom Fatigue requires that we insert more animated dialogue in varied ways into our virtual meetings. Second, we need to show up "larger than life" in our delivery so it conveys our dynamism across the screen pixelation.

As women, our three-dimensional persuasive selves *can* translate to the two-dimensional screen.

CHAPTER 11

Final Thoughts

W e women possess incredible power. In my dedication at the front of this book, I addressed the badass women who have come before us and who have been castigated for being aggressive when they were simply showing up as assertive. They were ahead of their time. We benefit from their courage, their brashness, their mistakes, and their triumphs.

And now, it's our time. We owe them, and we owe ourselves. Their behavior gave us momentum, and we are so much further ahead because of them. Today, we share equal credibility with men on so many fronts, and we excel in ways that emphasize our explosive power.

I want you to see your immense power and your ability to persuade both through the proven techniques contained in these pages and through your uniquely wonderful demeanor. Try these techniques, push yourself outside your comfort zone, adjust these approaches in ways that fit you, and reject what doesn't serve you.

Champion your fellow female colleagues and set the credibility bar high for the women and men who are watching. Now it's your turn to celebrate being badass.

And if you want my help in the form of a presentation or coaching, you can always reach me at karenlisko.com.

ENDNOTES

1   Adam Grant, "Women Know Exactly What They're Doing When They Use Weak Language," *The New York Times,* July 31, 2023, https://www.ny-times.co/2023/07/31/opinion/women-language-work.html?unlocked_article_code=1.ok4._pvD.nBrL3iRa_LKy&smid=url-sharhttps://www.ny-times.co/2023/07/31/opinion/women-language-work.html?unlocked_article_code=1.ok4._pvD.nBrL3iRa_LKy&smid=url-share.
2   Grant, July 31, 2023.
3   *Shark Tank,* September 21, 2012. Season 4, Episode 2.
4   Karen Ohnemus Lisko, "Juror Perceptions of Witness Credibility as a Function of Linguistic and Nonverbal Power," doctoral dissertation, 1992, https://hdl.handle.net/1808/30273.
5   Shanthi Manian & Ketki Sheth, "Follow My Lead: Assertive Cheap Talk and the Gender Gap," *Management Science* 67, no. 11 (February 17, 2021), https://doi.org/10.1287/mnsc.2020.3837.
6   Sophia Ruijun Liu, "Gendered Science Communications: The Role of Speaker Gender & Pitch in Perceived Credibility and Persuasion of Climate Science," Honors Thesis, University of Pennsylvania, 2022.

7   Deborah Jordan Brooks and Danny Hayes, "How Messages About Gender Bias Can Both Help and Hurt Women's Representation," *American Politics Research* 47, no. 3 (2019), https://doi.org/10.1177/1532673X18795608.

8   World Economic Forum, *World Economic Forum Annual Report* 2023-24, September 9, 2024, https://www.weforum.org/publications/annual-report-2023-2024.

9   Joseph Henrich, Steven J. Heine, and Ara Norenzayan, "The Weirdest People in the World?" *Behavioral and Brain Sciences* 33, no. 2 (2010): 1–75, https://doi.org/10.1017/S0140525X0999152X.

10 Mustafa Salari Rad, Alison Jane Martingano, and Jeremy Ginges, "Toward a Psychology of Homo Sapiens: Making Psychological Science More Representative of the Human Population," *Psychological and Cognitive Sciences* 115, no. 45 (2018): 11401–11405, https://doi.org/10.1073/pnas.1721165115.

11 Erin Meyer, *The Culture Map: Breaking Through the Invisible Boundaries of Global Business* (PublicAffairs, 2014).

12 Sui Sui, Horatio M. Morgan, and Matthias Baum, "Differences Between Women- and Men-Owned Export Businesses," *Journal of Small Business and Entrepreneurship* 34, no. 5 (March 3, 2022): 578–595, https://doi.org/10.1080/08276331.2022.2045169.

13 Nalini Ambady, "The Perils of Pondering: Intuition and Thin Slice Judgments," *Psychological Inquiry* 21, no. 4, (2010): 271–278, https://www.jstor.org/stable/25767201.

14 Dena Patton, *The Greatness Game: Inspired Ways to Live, Love, and Lead Like You Mean It* (Dena Patton LLC, 2017).

15 Raymond A. Mar, Jingyuan Li, Anh T.P. Nguyen, and Cindy P. Ta, "Memory and Comprehension of Narrative Versus Expository Texts: A Meta-Analysis." *Psychonomic Bulletin and Review* 28 (2021): 732–749, https://doi.org/10.3758/s13423-020-01853-1.

16 The early fairy tales followed a predictable formula of the hero (usually a man) saving the heroine (usually a woman). And let's not forget that only happy times permanently ensued once they kissed. Ha! Thankfully, modern plots created by Disney and Pixar often portray the heroine using her own power to save herself rather than needing a man to save her. Hallelujah.

17 Sally Perkins, *Noble Cause, Noble Story* (work in progress) (Niche Pressworks, publishing expected in 2025).

18 Importantly, starting with your *What* is a culturally significant (and very American) way of communicating. In her book, *The Culture Map* (PublicAffairs, 2014), Erin Meyer notes that bottom lining your point at the beginning is an applications-first model preferred by most Western European countries. Many other cultures follow a different model called "principles first," wherein they first provide their reasoning *before* they provide their bottom-line point. Consider your audience's cultural preferences before using the Triple W or What/Why/Where approach.

19 Stephen E. Toulmin, *The Uses of Argument (Updated Edition)* (Cambridge University Press, 2003).

20 Amy M. Do, Alexander V. Rupert, and George Wolford, "Evaluations of Pleasurable Experiences: The Peak-End Rule. *Psychonomic Bulletin & Review* 15, (2008): 96–98, https://doi.org/10.3758/PBR.15.1.96.

21 Carlos Sáenz-Royo, Francisco Chiclana, and Enrique Herrera-Viedma, "Steering Committee Management. Expertise, Diversity, and Decision-Making Structures," *Information Fusion* 99 (2023), https://doi.org/10.1016/j.inffus.2023.101888.

22 Asking a client, "What else?" rather than, "Is there anything else?" has the power to change the answer to the question. "What else?" calls for an open-ended disclosure from the client. "Is there anything else?" simply requires a close-ended "yes" or "no."

23 Ana Catalano Weeks and Leah Ruppanner, "A Typology of US Parents' Mental Loads: Core and Episodic Cognitive Labor," *Journal of Marriage and Family* (December 12, 2024), https://doi.org/10.1111/jomf.13057.

24 This is my variation of a quote from Maya Angelou. In its original form, Maya Angelou said, "People will forget what you said, people will forget what you did, but people will never forget how you made them feel."

25 Emma Rodero, Lluís Mas, and María Blanco, "The Influence of Prosody on Politicians' Credibility," *Journal of Applied Linguistics and Professional Practice* 11, no. 1 (2019): 89-111, https://doi.org/10.1558/japl.32411.

26 Lea E. Gikas and Zachary T. Sutcliffe, "The Effect of Vocal Fillers on Credibility, Communication Competence, and Likeability," *Communication Studies* (2019), https://digitalcommons.calpoly.edu/comssp/239.

27 Jean E. Fox Tree and Josef C. Schrock, "Discourse Markers in Spontaneous Speech: Oh What a Difference an Oh Makes," *Journal of Memory and Language* 40, no. 2 (1999): 280–295, doi:10.1006/jmla.1998.2613.

28 Karen Ohnemus Lisko, "Juror Perceptions of Witness Credibility as a Function of Linguistic and Nonverbal Power," Doctoral Dissertation (The University of Kansas, 1992), https://hdl.handle.net/1808/30273.

29 Emma Rodero, Lluís Mas, and María Blanco, "The Influence of Prosody on Politicians' Credibility," *Journal of Applied Linguistics and Professional Practice* 11, no. 1 (2019): 89–111, https://doi.org/10.1558/japl.32411; I.M. Latu and M. Schmid Mast, "Male interviewers' nonverbal dominance predicts lower evaluations of female applicants in simulated job interviews," *Journal of Personnel Psychology* 15, no. 3 (2016): 116–124, https://doi.org/10.1027/1866-5888/a000159.

30 Casey A. Klofstad, "Candidate Voice Pitch Influences Election Outcomes," *Political Psychology* 37, no. 5 (2015): 725–738. https://doi.org/10.1111/pops.12280; Alice Zoghaib, "The contribution of a brand spokesperson's voice to consumer-based brand equity," *The Journal of Product and Brand Management* 26, no. 5, (2017): 492–502, https://doi.org/10.1108/JPBM-06-2016-1230; Alice Zoghaib, "Persuasion of Voices: The Effects of a Speaker's Voice Characteristics and Gender on Consumers' Responses," *Research and Applications in Marketing* 34, no. 3 (2019): 83–110, https://doi.org/10.1177/2051570719828687.

31 Sophia (Ruijun) Liu, "Gendered Science Communication: The Role of Speaker Gender and Pitch in Perceived Credibility and Persuasion of Climate Science," Honors Thesis, University of Pennsylvania, 2022.

32 Pierre Habasque, "'You'll Never Have to Listen to Her Talk Like This? With an Upward Inflection? At the End of Every Sentence?' Fundamental Frequency of Female Voices and Linguistic Misogyny in Fox's *Family Guy*," *Anglophonia* 27 (2019), doi. org/10.4000/anglophonia.2352.

33 Emma Rodero, Olatz Larrea, Isabel Rodrigues de Dios, and Ignacio Lucas, "The Expressive Balance Effect, Perception and Physiological Responses of Prosody and Gestures," *Journal of Language and Social Psychology* 41, no. 6 (February 25, 2022), https://doi. org/10.1177/0261927X221078317.

34 Ashley E. Thompson and Daniel Voyer, "Sex Differences in the Ability to Recognise Non-Verbal Displays of Emotion: A Meta-Analysis," *Cognition and Emotion* 28, no. 7 (2014): 1164–95, doi:10.1080/02699931.2013.875889.

35 Lawrence Ian Reed, Rachel Stratton, and Jessica D. Rambeas, "Face Value and Cheap Talk: How Smiles Can Increase or Decrease the Credibility of Our Words," *Evolutionary Psychology* 16, no. 4 (2018), https://doi.org/10.1177/1474704918814400.

36 Silvia Bonaccio, Jane O'Reilly, Sharon L. O'Sullivan, and Francois Chiocchio, "Nonverbal Behavior and Communication in the Workplace: A Review and an Agenda for Research," *Journal of Management* 42, no. 5 (2016): 1044–1074, https://doi. org/10.1177/0149206315621146.

37 Li Huang, Adam D. Galinsky, Deborah H. Gruenfeld, and Lucia E. Guillory, "Powerful Postures Versus Powerful Roles: Which Is the Proximate Correlate of Thought and Behavior?" *Psychological Science* 22, no. 1 (2010) https://doi.org/10.1177/0956797610391912.

38 Yaping Gong, Siu-Yin Cheung, Mo Wang, and Jia-Chi Huang, "Unfolding the Proactive Process for Creativity: Integration of the Employee Proactivity, Information Exchange, and Psychological Safety Perspectives," *Journal of Management* 38, no. 5 (2012): 1611–1633, https://doi.org/10.1177/0149206310380250.

39 Li Huang, Adam D. Galinsky, Deborah H. Gruenfeld, and Lucia E. Guillory, "Powerful Postures Versus Powerful Roles: Which Is the Proximate Correlate of Thought and Behavior?" *Psychological Science* 22, no. 1 (2010), https://doi.org/10.1177/0956797610391912.

40 Cuddy, Amy. "Your Body Language May Shape Who You Are," TED Talk Global, October 1, 2012, Video, 20:12, https://www.ted.com/talks/amy_cuddy_your_body_language_may_shape_who_you_are.

41 Emma Rodero, Olatz Larrea, Isabel Rodrigues de Dios, and Ignacio Lucas, "The Expressive Balance Effect, Perception and Physiological Responses of Prosody and Gestures," *Journal of Language and Social Psychology* 41, no. 6 (February 25, 2022), https://doi.org/10.1177/0261927X221078317.

42 Elizabeth Hampson, Sari M. van Anders, and Lucy I. Mullin, "A Female Advantage in the Recognition of Emotional Facial Expressions: Test of an Evolutionary Hypothesis," *Evolution and Human Behavior* 27,

no. 6 (2006): 401–416, https://doi.org/10.1016/j.
evolhumbehav.2006.05.002.

43 Max Weisbuch, and Nalini Ambady, "Thin-Slice
Vision," *The Science of Social Vision*, Oxford Series in
Visual Cognition, Oxford Academic (2011), https://doi.
org/10.1093/acprof:oso/9780195333176.003.0014.

44 Antonela Kapitanović, Andrea Tokić, and Nataša
Šimić, "Differences in the Recognition of Sadness,
Anger, and Fear in Facial Expressions: The Role of the
Observer and Model Gender," *Archive for Industrial
Hygiene and Toxicology* 73, no. 4 (2022): 308–313,
https://doi.org/10.2478/aiht-2022-73-3662.

45 Nadine Aburumman, Marco Gillies, Jamie A. Ward,
and Antonia F. de C. Hamilton, "Nonverbal
Communication in Virtual Reality: Nodding as a
Social Signal in Virtual Interactions," *International
Journal of Human-Computer Studies* 164 (2022), https://
doi.org/10.1016/j.ijhcs.2022.102819.

46 Stefan Schulz-Hardt, Felix C. Brodbeck, Andreas
Mojzisch, Rudolf Kerschreiter, and Dieter Frey, "Group
Decision Making in Hidden Profile Situations: Dissent
as a Facilitator for Decision Quality," *Journal of
Personality and Social Psychology* 91, no. 6 (2006): 1080–
1093, https://doi.org/10.1037/0022-3514.91.6.1080.

47 Rachel Kleinfeld, "Polarization, Democracy, and
Political Violence in the United States: What
the Research Says," Carnegie Endowment for
International Peace (September 5, 2023), https://carne-
gie-production-assets.s3.amazonaws.com/static/files/
Kleinfeld_Polarization_final_3.pdf.

48 Lynn Vavrek, "A Measure of Identity: Are You Wedded to Your Party?" *The New York Times,* January 31, (2017, https://www.nytimes.com/2017/01/31/upshot/are-you-married-to-your-party.html.

49 Steve Kornacki, *The Red and the Blue: The 1990s and the Birth of Political Triablism* (Harper Collins, 2018).

50 Kenji Yoshino and David Glasgow, *Say the Right Thing: How to Talk About Identity, Diversity, and Justice* (Atria Books, 2023).

51 Yoshino and Glasgow, *Say the Right Thing.*

52 A deeper description of the20/60/20 principle appears in Dolly Chugh, *The Person You Mean to Be: How Good People Fight Bias* (Harper Business, 2022). She makes the point that the percentages are somewhat arbitrary. Other researchers suggest the percentage of the "unmovable" is closer to 30 percent. See D. Westen, *The Political Brain: The Role of Emotion in Deciding the Fate of the Nation* (PublicAffairs, 2008). The point is that the "movable middle" is the largest percentage.

53 William Ury, *The Power of a Positive No: How to Say No and Still Get to Yes* (Bantam Books, 2007), p. 55.

54 Mark Murphy, *Managing Narcissists, Blamers, Dramatics, and More... Research-Driven Scripts for Managing Difficult Personalities at Work* (Mark Murphy: 2019).

55 See R. Brinkman and R. Kirschner, *Dealing with People You Can't Stand: How to Bring Out the Best in People at Their Worst* (McGraw-Hill, 2024), M. Murphy, *Managing Narcissists, Blamers, Dramatics, and More,* and W. Lundin, K, Lundin, and M. Dobson, *Working with Difficult People* (American Marketing Association, 2009).

56 Brinkman and Kirschner, *Dealing with People You Can't Stand*, p. 29.

57 Murphy, *Managing Narcissists,* p. 88.

58 Brinkman and Kirschner, *Dealing with People You Can't Stand*.

59 Ibid.

60 Ibid.

61 Jarad Cooney Horvath, "The Neuroscience of PowerPoint," *Mind, Brain, and Education* 8, no. 3 (2014): 137–143, https://doi.org/10.1111/mbe.12052.

62 Geraldine Fauville, Mufan Luo, Anna Carolina Muller Queiroz, Jeremy N. Bailenson, and Jeff Hancock, "Zoom Exhaustion and Fatigue Scale," *Computers in Human Behaviors Report* 4 (2021), https://doi.org/10.1016/j.chbr.2021.100119.

63 Geraldine Fauville, Mufan Luo, Anna Carolina Muller Queiroz, Lee, A., Jeremy N. Bailenson, and Jeff Hancock, "Video-Conferencing Usage Dynamics and Nonverbal Mechanisms Exacerbate Zoom Fatigue, Particularly for Women," *Computers in Human Behaviors Report* 10 (2023), https://doi.org/10.1016/j.chbr.2023.100271.

64 Slido, accessed February 10, 2025, www.slido.com.

65 Stefan Schulz-Hardt, Felix C. Brodbeck, Andreas Mojzisch, Rudolf Kerschreiter, and Dieter Frey, "Group Decision Making in Hidden Profile Situations: Dissent as a Facilitator for Decision Quality," *Journal of Personality and Social Psychology* 91, no. 6 (2006): 1080–1093, https://doi.org/10.1037/0022-3514.91.6.1080.

66 Patrick M. Lencioni, *Death by Meeting: A Leadership Fable About Solving the Most Painful Problem in Business* (Jossey-Bass, 2004).

67 For something important (and often counterintuitive) like this list, consider sharing your screen in an online meeting to post these rules *every time.* Research how you can do this without shrinking the gallery view of your attendees in your given platform. There are ways to make the rules a "meeting attendee" that doesn't overpower the real estate of your screen.

68 You can find out more about this camera at huehd.com.

ACKNOWLEDGEMENTS

How do I thank and list the countless women and allied men who have contributed to these pages? Everything in this book comes from learning as much from my audiences as I believe they learned from me. It comes from reading the latest in research and getting to conduct my own. I'm a deeply fortunate human who has gotten to road-test the concepts I've taught you here over and over again. Without those terrific women giving me feedback along the way, this would have been a superficial effort. Instead, I hope it conveys depth and practicality.

As for this book-writing effort, oh my goodness. Niche Pressworks and its smart team of dedicated women (and men) are simply the best at what they do. They guided me (and held me accountable!) every step of the way. Nicole Gebhardt is at the helm and was instrumental in guiding me to shape my morass of thinking into a focused book plan. The Niche team included great coaches along the way: Dena Patton on greatness mindsets and storyteller Michael Hauge. Kim Han project managed me through the steps to help my overwhelm and to ensure I knew what the heck I was doing at every phase. And the Niche editorial team: Ellen gave me my reality check on the "big picture" of the book and did so with equal parts smarts and grace and Melanie was with me chapter to chapter, telling it to me straight when I was off-message and providing me with her gentle wisdom and writing smarts to get my messaging back on track. Melanie, you are Kind Dynamite.

To everyone at Niche, thank you. This book would have simply stayed swirling in my head as it had for years if not for you.

I must also acknowledge so many other smart, professional women in my life who may not even realize they have emulated the Kind Dynamite approach for years and, as a result, have become dear friends. You know who you are, and if I started listing you by name, it would take pages, or worse, I would inadvertently leave someone out. I will dedicate my plan to thanking you in person. But I will still call out my dear friends Sally Perkins and Marsha Graesser, who have been my writing sounding board for this book and my much-needed sanity (and sometimes hilarity) check along the way.

Finally, thank you to my beautiful family who has sacrificed time with me during this writing process and so many other work projects over the years. You cheered me on, nonetheless. My children are my heart — Elena, Alex, and Nika. And to my hands-down, number-one supporter and soul both in writing and in life, my husband, Brian.

ABOUT KAREN LISKO, PH.D.

Dr. Karen Lisko is a social scientist who spends her days coaching professionals to find their most persuasive authentic voices in settings that count. And, really, what setting doesn't? She draws upon three decades of experience from the boardroom to the courtroom and her doctorate in communication studies. As a communications consultant, she has spoken to thousands of professionals in small companies and in Fortune 10 and Fortune 500 corporations both in person and virtually. Her deep passion is grounded in working with professional women and women's organizations in the United States and internationally. As a trial consultant, she has been awarded the greatest honor bestowed by The American Society of Trial Consultants as the recipient of the 2024 Lifetime Achievement Award.

Dr. Lisko lives in Phoenix near her three talkative, grown children and with her husband, who can barely get a word in edgewise. When she isn't sweating in the Arizona heat, she is sweating in a hot yoga studio — all by choice.

Contact

Website:	KarenLisko.com
Email:	Karen@KarenLisko.com
LinkedIn:	KarenLisko
Facebook:	DrKarenLisko
Instagram:	@DrKarenLisko

www.ingramcontent.com/pod-product-compliance
Lightning Source LLC
Chambersburg PA
CBHW071602210326
41597CB00019B/3360